IMPRESSUM

Roger Hassler (Hrsg.):
Airbrush Bodypainting Step by Step. Hamburg 2009.
ISBN-13: 978-3-941656-01-7
Text + Konzept: Roger Hassler, Katja Hassler
Redaktionsassistenz + Lektorat: Ragna Pfeiffer
Layout + Satz: Lisa Bruchwitz, Galina Wunder
Übersetzung: Martina Ledlova
Umschlag-Fotos von: Roger Hassler (Bodypainting),
Claus Döpelheuer, istockphoto, Mist-Air, Temptu

© 2009, newart medien & design GbR
Katja + Roger Hassler
Tratzigerstr. 21
22043 Hamburg
www.newart.de

IMPRINT

Roger Hassler (ed.):
Airbrush Bodypainting Step by Step. Hamburg 2009.
ISBN-13: 978-3-941656-01-7
Text + Concept: Roger Hassler, Katja Hassler
Editorial assistant + editorial office: Ragna Pfeiffer
Layout + Set-Up: Lisa Bruchwitz, Galina Wunder
Translation: Martina Ledlova
Cover Photos by: Roger Hassler (body painting),
Claus Döpelheuer, istockphoto, Mist-Air, Temptu

© 2009, newart medien & design GbR
Katja + Roger Hassler
Tratzigerstr. 21
22043 Hamburg
www.newart.de

INHALTSVERZEICHNIS

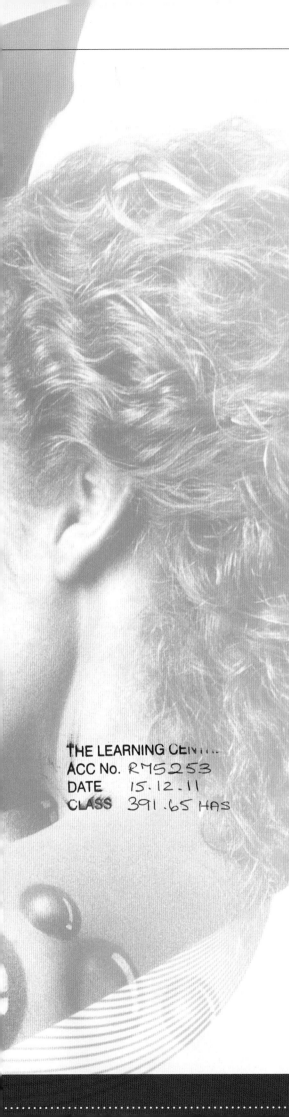

TABLE OF CONTENTS

FASZINATION
BODYPAINTING
Herausforderung Airbrush

FASCINATION BODY PAINTING
Airbrush challenge

DAS BEMALEN DES KÖRPERS mit farbigen Materialien gibt es in der Menschheitsgeschichte schon seit Urzeiten. In vielen sogenannten „primitiven Kulturen" ist es heute noch üblich, zu besonderen Anlässen und Zeremonien den Körper mit Farbe zu schmücken. Die Farbe kann Ausdruck von Freude sein, sie kann aber auch zur Abschreckung von Feinden oder bösen Geistern dienen. Die bekanntesten Beispiele dafür in der westlichen Welt sind wahrscheinlich die Kriegsbemalungen der Indianer oder die noch bis in die heutige Zeit reichende Bemalung eines Clowns.

PAINTING HUMAN BODIES with colourful substances has been heard of in the history of humankind already from time immemorial. In many so called "primitive cultures", body painting is still common today as a way of decorating human bodies with paint on special occasions and ceremonies. The colour can be an expression of joy but it can also serve to ward off the enemies or evil spirits. The most famous examples found in the western world are probably the warrior make-up designs of the Indians or the clown´s make-up.

In allen Fällen wird die Bemalung des Körpers jedoch dazu eingesetzt, den Ausdruck, die Stimmung, Bewegung oder Form des menschlichen Körpers besonders zu betonen. Auch die modernen Formen des Bodypaintings – seien es bemalte Kindergesichter am Geburtstag, mit National- oder Vereinsflaggen geschmückte Körper von Fußball-Fans oder künstlerisch inszenierte Ganzkörper-Bodypaintings bei Festivals und Events – haben letztlich den Anspruch, die Ästhetik des Körpers zu unterstreichen und auf eine bestimmte Weise zu interpretieren.

In all these cases, the painting on the body draws a bead on a unicolor accentuation of expression, mood, movement or shape of the human body. Also the modern forms of body painting – be it the painted faces of children at some birthday party, bodies of football fans decorated with national or club flags, or the artistically staged whole body paintings at festivals and events – are entitled to underscore the aesthetics of the body and to interpret these in a particular way.

Es ist sicherlich davon auszugehen, dass in westlichen Kulturen heutzutage ein gewisser Reiz des Bodypaintings – insbesondere des Ganzkörper-Bodypaintings – von der Nacktheit des Körpers ausgeht. Provokation durch Nacktheit und verändertes Aussehen gehört in einigen Bereichen zu den – gewollten oder ungewollten – Wirkungen des Bodypaintings.

Nowadays we can certainly take for granted that in the western cultures, a certain appeal of body painting – and in particular of the whole body painting – arises from the nudity. In some fields, the provocation through nudity and changed looks belongs to the – desired or unwanted – effects of body painting.

Für Künstler und Auftraggeber dagegen liegt die Faszination in erster Linie in den Ausdrucksmöglichkeiten und der Kurzlebigkeit des Werkes.

Im Gegensatz zur traditionellen Kunst auf Leinwand und Papier ist das Bodypainting-Kunstwerk lebendig. Wie jeder Mensch, so ist auch jedes Bodypainting einzigartig. Mit jeder Bewegung und Pose verändert es sich. Bildende (Malerei, Plastik) und darstellende Künste (Tanz, Schauspielerei) verbinden sich im Kunstwerk auf faszinierende Weise. Und eine weitere Kunst gehört oft dazu: Die Fotografie. Sie überwindet die Kurzlebigkeit des Kunstwerks, indem sie das oft nur wenige Stunden existierende Bodypainting für die Ewigkeit festhält und in Szene setzt.

However, for the artists and ordering customers the fascination is primarily due to the possibilities of expression and to the ephemerality of the work.

Opposite to the traditional art on canvas and paper, the body painting artwork is alive. As every human being, every body painting is just one of its kind. It is changing with every movement and pose. Fine arts (painting and plastic arts) and performing arts (dancing, acting) band together fascinatingly united in an artwork. And another art belongs to it: the photography. It overcomes the ephemerality of the artwork to put it – the artwork that often only exists for a couple of hours – on a durable stage for ever.

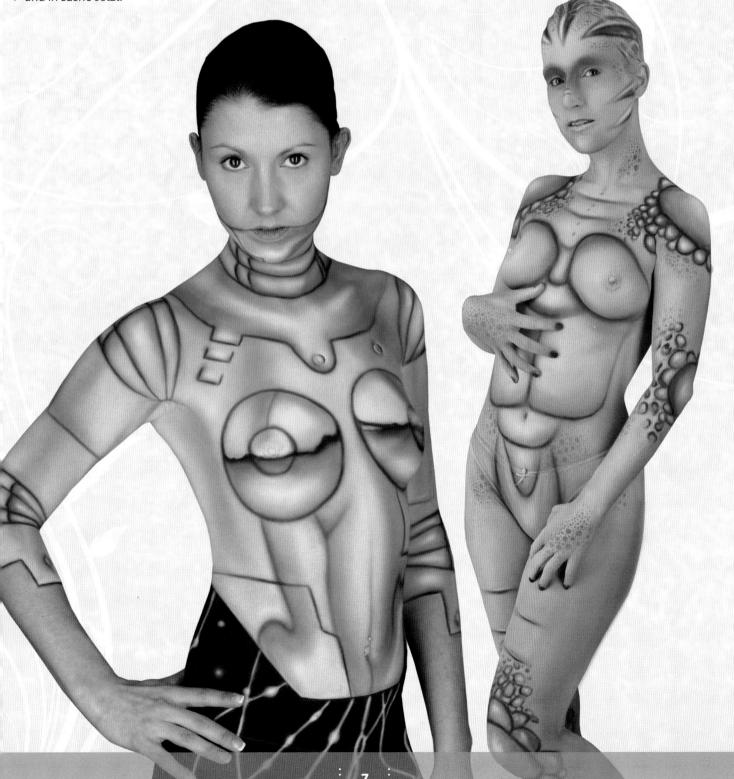

Anwendungsbereiche und Motive

Die Anlässe und Anwendungsbereiche des Bodypaintings sind heutzutage ebenso vielseitig wie seine Motive. Je nach Anlass kann es sich dabei um einfarbige Grundierungen, strukturierte Muster, Logos und Schriftzüge oder ganze figürliche Kunstwerke handeln.

Events

Bei Veranstaltungen sind Bodypaintings immer wieder beliebte Hingucker. Firmen nutzen Bodypaintings gerne zur sinnlichen Präsentation ihrer Produkte. Promotion-Girls werden dann mit Logos und Schriftzügen versehen oder erhalten einfach ein aufsehenerregendes Design, das zum angebotenen Produkt passt.

Auch als Live-Event sind Bodypaintings beliebt, so dass sie häufig neben Tanz- und Musikperformances zum Rahmenprogramm von Messen oder Festivals gehören.

Range of Application and Motifs

The occasions and fields of application of body painting are nowadays just as versatile as their motifs. According to an occasion, there might be unicolor basecoats, structured patterns, logos and texts, or whole figurative artworks.

Events

Body paintings are always a popular eye-catcher at events. Companies are fond of using body paintings to sensuously present their products. Promoting girls are than decorated with logos and texts, or they are simply covered in a spectacular design that suits the product on offer.

Body paintings are also popular as live events and belong often to the main program at trade fairs and festivals accompanying dance and music performances.

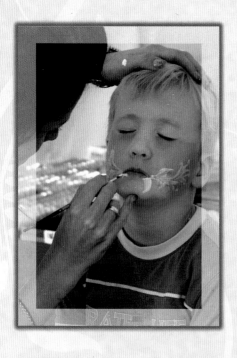

Innerhalb einer halben bis einer Stunde entsteht dabei vor den Augen der Zuschauer ein Bodypainting, das sich meistens durch einfache, aber effektvolle Motive wie z.B. die Imitation von Kleidungsstücken oder Material- (Holz, Metall, Stein) oder Fellstrukturen auszeichnet.

„Bodypaintings für jedermann" sind Airbrush-Tattoos oder Kinderschminkaktionen, die bei Straßenfesten, Gartenparties oder Messen kostenlos oder für 1 bis 5 Euro angeboten werden. Für Bodypainting-Künstler sind Events auf jeden Fall gute Einnahmequellen – egal ob hauptberuflich oder zur Aufbesserung des „Taschengeldes".

Within half an hour to an hour, body paintings, which mostly feature simple but impressive motifs such as imitation of clothes or materials (wood, metal, stone) or fur structures, emerge right in front of the eyes of an audience.

"Body paintings for everyone" are airbrush tattoos or make-up happenings provided to children at street parties, garden parties or trade fairs for free or sometimes for 1 to 5 Euro. For body painting artists, such events are definitely good sources of income – no matter if it is their regular occupation or just an improvement of their "pocket money".

Kunst

Das künstlerische Bodypainting ist sozusagen die Königsdisziplin. Diese Werke können abstrakt sein und einfach aus interessanten Farb- und Formenkompositionen bestehen oder aber auch figürliche Teile enthalten. Künstlerisches Bodypainting kann entweder der Live-Präsentation dienen, z.B. auf den nationalen und internationalen Bodypainting-Festivals, oder aber Motiv eines Fotoshootings werden, um es später in Büchern, Zeitschriften, Postern, Kalender o.ä. zu veröffentlichen.

Künstlerische Bodypaintings sind meist Gesamtkunstwerke, bei denen die Performance, der Hintergrund sowie weitere Accessoires mit dem Bodypainting zusammen konzipiert werden.

Art

The artistic body painting is recognized to be the supreme discipline. These artworks can be abstract and consist simply of interesting colour and shape compositions, but also they can embody figurative elements. The artistic body painting can serve either the live presentation, for example at the national and international body painting festivals, or it can be a subject to a photo shooting session so to make it accessible for publication in books, magazines, posters, calendars or the like.

Artistic body paintings are mostly complete artworks for which the performance, the background as well as other accessories shall be worked out contiguously.

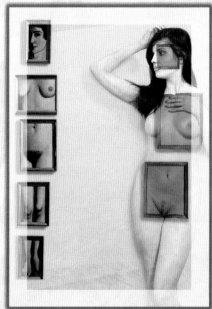

So umfasst z.B. jede Bodypainting-Präsentation auf einem Festival die individuelle Gestaltung der Frisur, u.U. zum Motiv passende Requisiten, darauf abgestimmte Musik und schauspielerische, tänzerische oder akrobatische Einlagen des Modells. Fotoshootings finden dagegen häufig in ungewöhnlichen Kulissen statt oder der Künstler gestaltet selber Hintergründe, die zu seinem Bodypainting passen. Hinzu kommt die Inszenierung von Licht und Pose, die der Fotograf zusammen mit Künstler und Modell arrangiert.

In diesem Zusammenhang gibt es klassische Bodypainting-Motive wie z.B. „Camouflage"-Effekte, bei denen das Modell in einem natürlichen Hintergrund (z.B. einer Mauer) quasi verschwindet. Bodypainting-Festivals geben den Künstlern dagegen Themen vor, zu denen sie ihr Modell gestalten müssen. Manche Künstler verwenden ihr Modell dabei als Leinwand, auf die sie figürliche Motive aufbringen. Andere dagegen gestalten ihr Modell z.B. zu einem einheitlichen Wesen (Monster, Roboter, Meerjungfrau o.ä.).

As a result, for example each body painting presentation at a festival includes an individual hair design, possibly the motif-matching props and music, acting, dancing or acrobatic contributions of the model. In contrast, photo shootings often take place in an unusual coulisse or the artist himself designs the backgrounds that match his body painting. In addition to this, the photographer together with the artist and the model arrange the staging of light and pose.

Of course, there are the classical body painting motifs, for example "camouflage"-effects, which make the model virtually disappear in the natural background (such as a wall). Body painting festivals, on the opposite, define the themes according to which the artists must design their models. Some artists use the model widely as a canvas and create figurative motifs on their bodies whereas others design their models to create a complete character (for example a monster, androids, mermaids or the like).

Film und Fernsehen

Die Anwendung des Bodypaintings in Film und Fernsehen hat vor allem kosmetische Zwecke und gehört in den Bereich der Maskenbildnerei. Ein großer Bereich ist natürlich die Gestaltung von Fantasiegestalten, z.B. bei Filmen wie „Harry Potter", „Herr der Ringe" oder „Star Trek". Dort werden zusammen mit Special Effects-Techniken Masken, Haut- und Körperteile appliziert, um die menschliche Gestalt zu verändern. Hautfarben werden verändert, Falten, Strukturen und Schattierungen aufgemalt. Trotz zunehmender digitaler Tricktechnik sind „handgestaltete" Darsteller noch immer unentbehrlich.

Insbesondere der Airbrush-Technik kommt darüber hinaus die Entwicklung der hochauflösenden Kameratechnik HDTV zu Gute: Aufgrund der klaren und scharfen Bilder macht diese Aufnahmemethode jedes zu viel aufgetragene Farbpigment sichtbar, so dass das Airbrushgerät ganz allmählich Pinsel und Puderquaste aus den Garderoben von TV-Studios und Filmsets verbannt. Nicht nur für Special Effects, sondern auch für die normale hauttonfarbene Foundation wird inzwischen die Spritzpistole verwendet.

Movie and Television

Using body paintings in the movies and television results especially out of the cosmetic purposes and belongs into the field of mask-building and make-up. One huge field is the design of phantasy characters, for example for movies such as "Harry Potter", "Lord of the Rings" or "Star Trek". For these, the application of special effects, make-up, skin and body parts merge to alter the whole of the human being. Skin tones are changed, and wrinkles, structures and shadings are painted. Regardless the increasing popularity of digital trick techniques, the "handmade" actors have still remained indispensable.

In particular, the airbrush technique benefits from the development of the HDTV camera: As a consequence of clear, sharp pictures, every in excess applied colour pigment is visible so that the airbrush device by and by banishes the paintbrushes and the puff from the dressing rooms of TV studios and movie sets. Meanwhile, the airbrush has been put into service not only for the special effects, but also for the normal skin-tone coloured foundation.

Bodypainting Techniken

Seit jeher gibt es verschiedenste Techniken für die Körperbemalung: Ursprünglich wurden Naturfarben natürlich mit den Händen aufgetragen, aber auch Holzstöcke wie z.B. bei Henna-Bemalungen kamen zum Einsatz. Heute gehören Pinsel, Schwamm und Airbrush zu den Hauptwerkzeugen des professionellen Bodypaintings, für den Laien gibt es zum Karneval, für Kindergeburtstage oder andere Anlässe auch Schminkstifte und Kreiden.

Jede Technik hat ihren individuellen Reiz, Vor- und Nachteile: Das Auftragen der Farbe mit den Händen ist sicherlich zum Kinderschminken gut geeignet und kann auch einen sinnlichen Reiz haben. Pinsel und Schwamm sowie auch Kreiden und Stifte sind klassische Mal- und Schminkutensilien, die jeder Mensch schon einmal in der Hand gehabt hat. Umso leichter lässt sich hier der Zugang zum Bodypainting finden. Das nötige Equipment ist klein, leicht und preisgünstig. Darüber hinaus ist die Auswahl an Farben sowie ihre Verfügbarkeit im Vergleich zur Airbrush-Technik wesentlich größer. Jeder Drogerie-Markt führt heute schon Schminkfarben in Puder-, Stift- oder Pastenform, zumindest in den Grundfarben, die den Einstieg ins Bodypainting ermöglichen.

Body Painting Techniques

There always have been different techniques of body painting: Originally, the natural paints were commonly applied with hands, or sometimes with woodblocks such as in the case of henna paintings. Nowadays, paintbrush, sponge and airbrush belong to the essential equipment of the body painting profession. For the layman there are make-up pens and chalks that can be easily used for carnivals, children's birthdays or other occasions.

Each technique exercises its individual attraction, and of course has its pros and cons: Application of paint with hands is certainly well suitable for children's make-up. It also can be sensuously appealing. However, paintbrush and sponge as well as chalks and pens are the more traditional painting and make-up utensils that everybody has held in the hand at least once yet. The easier it is to follow the path leading to body painting. The necessary equipment is small, light-weight and low priced. Furthermore, the assortment of paints as well as their availability are much better when compared to the airbrush technique. Nowadays every chemist offers make-up paints in powder, pen or paste form at least as far as in the basic colours which enable anybody to enter the world of body painting.

Airbrush-Bodypainting

Die Airbrush-Technik ist die jüngste und auch „technisierteste" Methode der Körperbemalung. Sie hat einen grundlegenden Unterschied zu allen anderen Maltechniken: Der Farbauftrag funktioniert absolut berührungsfrei; das Airbrushgerät gleitet stets in einem Mindestabstand von wenigen Millimetern am Körper entlang und verteilt die Farbe mit einem leichten Luftzug auf der Haut. Von den meisten Modellen wird diese Technik als sehr angenehm wahrgenommen, obgleich oftmals auch erste Vorbehalte und Berührungsängste gegenüber dem fremden Gerät im Spiel sind.

Künstlerisch betrachtet ist die Airbrush-Technik insbesondere wegen ihres gleichmäßigen, schnellen und dünnen Farbauftrags beliebt. Richtig angewendet ist die Farbe auf dem Körper sofort trocken; aufgrund der dünnen Farbschicht gibt es weniger Farbverkrustungen, die aufbrechen oder die Bewegungsfreiheit des Modells einschränken könnten. Dieser Eigenschaft ist es zu verdanken, dass sich die Airbrush derzeit auch als Schminkwerkzeug beim hochauflösenden HD-Film und -Fernsehen durchsetzt.

Darüber hinaus bietet die Technik erstaunliche Ausdrucksmöglichkeiten wie z.B. das Arbeiten mit Schablonen und Maskierungen, um harte Kanten zu erzeugen, die Gestaltung von weichen Farbübergängen und Schattierungen, die ein Motiv besonders realistisch aussehen lassen, und die Erzeugung von anderen Effekten wie z.B. Farbsprenkeln oder sich wiederholende Muster.

Kehrseite dieses ungewöhnlichen Werkzeugs ist jedoch seine spezielle Handhabung, die von dem Anwender viel Übung verlangt und viele Bodypainter nicht selten davor zurückschrecken lässt. Viele Airbrush-Künstler haben etliche Jahre „Learning by doing" mit allen Höhen und Tiefen hinter sich. Denn es gibt nur vereinzelt Kursangebote, die gezielt Airbrush für Bodypainting vermitteln. Darüber hinaus gehört zur Airbrush-Technik ein ganzes Repertoire an Ausrüstung, das im Vergleich zu Pinsel, Schwamm und Stiften sowohl unhandlich als auch kostspielig und wartungsintensiv ist – angefangen bei einem Airbrushgerät (Qualitätsprodukte ab ca. 100 Euro), Kompressor (Einstiegsgeräte ab ca. 150 Euro) sowie diverses Ersatz- und Zubehörmaterial wie Düsen, Nadeln, Schläuche, Halterungen etc.

Nichts desto weniger hat sich die Airbrush-Pistole einen festen Platz in der Körperkunst erworben, so dass auch die seit rund 10 Jahren etablierten internationalen Bodypaintingfestivals Airbrush inzwischen neben Pinsel und Schwamm als eigenständige Wettbewerbskategorie führen.

Airbrush Body Painting

The airbrush technique is the youngest and at the same time the "most engineered" method of body painting. It fundamentally differs from all the other painting techniques: The application of paints happens without a single contact; the airbrush device slides always in a minimum distance of at least some millimetres from the body and dispenses the paint with a light airflow upon the skin. Most of the models perceive this technique as very pleasant, albeit there are often some initial reservations and fears of contact with the unfamiliar device playing their part.

From the artistic point of view, the airbrush technique is popular especially thanks to the even, fast and thin paint application. Used in the right manner, the paint dries on the body right away; due to the thin paint layer there are less paint crusts which could break or hinder the model´s movements. It is thanks to this feature that the airbrush has become a gladly accepted make-up tool also in the field of high definition movie and television.

Furthermore, the airbrush technique offers amazing expressive possibilities, for example through the work with stencils and masking to create sharp edges, soft colour gradients and shadings, which make a motif look particularly realistic, and the creation of other effects such as for example colour sprinkling or recurring patterns.

One drawback of this unusual tool is its special handling which requires some routine. Not rarely, this fact frightens off many bodypainters. Many airbrush artists look back on many years of "learning by doing" with all their ups and downs. And still, there are only sporadic courses specifically targeting the airbrush for body painting. Furthermore, the airbrush technique demands a wide repertoire of equipment which is – compared to the paintbrush, sponge and pens – both unhandy and sumptuous as well as maintenance-intensive – starting with an airbrush device (quality products from ca 100 €), compressor (starter models from ca 150 €) as well as diverse spare parts and auxiliary equipment such as nozzles, needles, hoses, clamps etc.

Nevertheless, the airbrush pistol has positioned itself very firmly in the body painting art so that also the international body painting festivals, that have been well established within the last 10 years, define airbrush as a self-contained competitive category next to the paintbrush and sponge.

AIRBRUSHES
im Überblick
Overview of
Airbrush Devices

DIE WECHSELVOLLE GESCHICHTE des Airbrushens begann bereits im späten 19. Jahrhundert, wo der Amerikaner Charles Burdick seine ausgetüftelte Konstruktion einer Spritzpistole als Patent anmeldete. Basierend auf den Ideen von Abner Peeler, Liberty und Charles Walkup und weiterentwickelt von Leuten wie Henry Thayer, Charles Chandler, Olaus Wold und Jens Paasche entstand in Europa und den USA zeitgleich ein brauchbares Werkzeug, welches sich bis heute in den Grundlagen kaum geändert hat: Durch die gleichzeitige Zufuhr von Luft und Farbe entsteht ein feiner regulierbarer Sprühstrahl, der es ermöglicht, Farbe sehr dünn, sogar transparent, aufzutragen und so gleichmäßige Farbflächen und Farbverläufe innerhalb kürzester Zeit anzulegen.

THE RICH HISTORY of airbrush has started already in the late 19th century as the American Charles Burdick filed his application for a patent for an airbrush pistol construction worked out right down to the smallest detail. Based on the ideas of Abner Peeler, Liberty and Charles Walkup, and further developed by people such as Henry Thayer, Charles Chandler, Olaus Wold and Jens Paasche, this very useful tool came into being in Europe and the USA at the same time. And indeed, it has not changed a lot in its basic features to this day: The concurrent feed of air and paint empower a fine, regulable spray jet, enabling the application of a very thin, even transparent paint layers, and the creation of even colour areas and colour gradients within a very short time.

BEDIENUNGSARTEN

Heute gibt es eine Vielzahl von unterschiedlichen Airbrushgeräten auf dem Markt. Unabhängig von Markennamen und Anwendungsgebieten lassen sie sich aus technischer Sicht in drei Grundtypen einteilen:

Single Action:
Airbrushgerät mit Einfachfunktion

Single Action Airbrushgeräte sind hinsichtlich ihres Aufbaus und ihrer Handhabung am einfachsten. Zu ihrer Verwendung muss lediglich der Farbauslösehebel nach unten gedrückt werden, um den Luft-Farb-Strahl ein- und auszuschalten. Ähnlich wie bei einer Sprühdose besteht dabei nicht die Möglichkeit, Farb- und Luftzufuhr individuell während der Anwendung zu regulieren. Aus diesem Grund eignet sich so ein Gerät nur, um großflächig Farbe aufzutragen wie z.B. beim Airbrush-Tanning (Ganzkörperbräunung) oder zur einfarbigen Grundierung des Körpers. Künstlerisches Bodypainting, Tattoos, Hair Art oder Airbrush-Make-up lassen sich damit nicht gestalten.

Double Action: Airbrushgerät
mit unabhängiger Doppelfunktion

Das Double Action System hat sich weltweit durchgesetzt und wird von schätzungsweise ca. 95 % aller Airbrushkünstler in den verschiedensten Bereichen – von der Illustration über Modellbau bis hin zu Auto- und Motorradlackierung sowie natürlich auch Bodypainting – verwendet. Das Gerät zeichnet sich dadurch aus, dass man mit dem Bedienhebel sowohl die Luftzufuhr als auch den Farbfluss regulieren kann. Durch Herunterdrücken des Hebels wird die Luftzufuhr aktiviert, durch Zurückziehen des Hebels kann die Farbzufuhr reguliert werden. Diese Doppelfunktion, die nur mit dem Zeigefinger bedient wird, erfordert anfänglich ein bißchen Übung und Fingerspitzengefühl, ermöglicht aber schließlich die genaue Dosierung der Farbe und die Erzeugung von Linienstärken von ganz fein bis „breit vernebelt".

HANDLING

Nowadays there are many different airbrush devices available on the market. Irrespective of brand names and fields of application, they can be divided into three basic groups from the technical perspective:

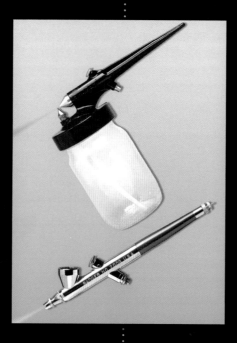

Single-Action: Airbrush
Device with Single Functionality

Single-action airbrush devices are the simplest case as to their construction and handling. To use these, i.e. to activate and deactivate the air-colour jet, the paint-release trigger simply must be pressed. Similar to a spray can, there is no possibility to regulate the paint and air feed individually during the application. That is why such a device is only appropriate for an application of large-scale paint areas such as e.g. airbrush tanning or a unicolor basecoat. It is not useful for the creation of artistic body paintings, tattoos, hair art or airbrush make-up.

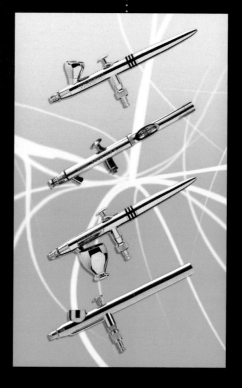

Double-Action: Airbrush Device with
Independent Double Functionality

The double-action system has become widely accepted worldwide and approximately 95% of all airbrush artists in the various fields use this device – ranging from the illustration, model building up to the car and bike lacquering and of course body painting. It stands out due to one control trigger to regulate the air feed as well as the paint feed. The air feed is activated through pressing the trigger and the paint feed can be regulated while pulling back the same trigger. This doubled functionality is run by only a forefinger and requires especially in the beginning some practice as well as a fine, instinctive feel. But it allows for a very exact dosage of the paint, the creation of line strength in the range from very fine till "wide oversprayed".

Kontrollierte Double Action:
Airbrushgerät mit abhängiger Doppelfunktion

Es gibt nur wenige Modelle auf dem Markt, die nach dem Prinzip der abhängigen Doppelfunktion arbeiten. Bei diesen Geräten lässt sich – wie bei dem Double-Action-Typ – die Farbmenge über den Hebel regulieren. Allerdings muss dieser nur zurückgezogen und nicht mehr nach unten gedrückt werden. Über das Zurückziehen des Hebels wird also zugleich die Luftzufuhr aktiviert und die Farbmenge reguliert. Diese Geräte eignen sich auch für das sehr detaillierte Arbeiten und werden oftmals von Einsteigern als leichter bedienbar eingestuft als Double Action Geräte. Im Bodypainting ist dieser Typ eher selten zu finden, ist aber letztlich genauso gut dafür geeignet wie ein Double Action Gerät. Wem diese Art der Bedienung besser liegt, kann diesen Typus beim Kauf also ebenso in Betracht ziehen.

Sondergeräte für besondere Anwendungen

Neben den genannten Standardtypen haben sich Hersteller im Laufe der Zeit natürlich auch individuelle Techniken einfallen lassen, um besondere Branchen und Anwendungsbereiche zu bedienen. Für den Kosmetikbereich wurden z.B. spezielle kleine Airbrushgeräte zum Auftragen von Airbrush-Make-up entwickelt. In Form, Größe und Design sind diese Geräte sozusagen direkt auf das Schminktäschchen abgestimmt. Technisch gesehen werden die kugelschreibergroßen Geräte von einem Mini-Kompressor mit Luft versorgt und versprühen per Knopfdruck (Single Action) das zuvor eingefüllte Make-up.

Natürlich lassen sich auch „verwandte" Spritzgeräte aus anderen Bereichen einsetzen – wie z.B. Lackierpistolen. Der Gedanke, einen Menschen wie ein Auto mit einer Lackierpistole zu bearbeiten, mag dem einen oder anderen sicherlich eine Gänsehaut verursachen. Dennoch lassen sich vor allem kleinere Industriepistolen gerade zum schnellen und gleichmäßigen „Grundieren" des Körpers sehr gut einsetzen. Lackierpistolen lassen sich durch ihren Zughebel besonders einfach bedienen und versprühen durch ihre vergleichsweise großen Düsen (z.T. von über 1 mm) in kurzer Zeit große Farbmengen.

Controlled Double-Action:
Airbrush Device with a Dependent Double Functionality

There are only few models on the market that work with a dependent double-action. With these devices, it is possible to regulate the paint feed – same as with the double-action model – with the control trigger. However, this trigger must be pulled back but does not need to be pressed in addition. Through pulling back the trigger, the air feed is activated and the paint feed can be regulated at the same time. These devices are also well suitable for working on detail and they are often classified by beginners as the ones with an easier handling when compared to double-action devices. This type is more seldom in the body painting but after all as suitable as the double-action devices. Who is more fond of this kind of handling might want to think about buying this kind of device.

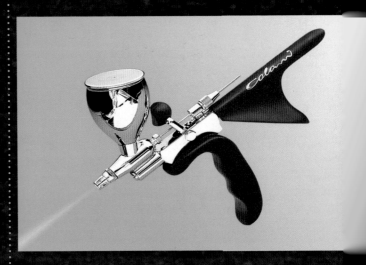

Special Devices for Special Purposes

Beside the above standard types, the manufacturers naturally came with some more individual techniques to serve special branches of trade and special spheres of application. For the cosmetic field companies produce special small airbrushes developed for the application of airbrush make-up. The form, size and design of these devices are adjusted to the make-up box. From the technical perspective, this device, as small as a pen, is fed air by a mini-compressor and sprays the make-up at the push of button.

It is of course possible to use also "related" devices from other fields – such as lacquer pistols. The idea of working on a human body with the same lacquer pistol as on the car can certainly give heebei-jeebies to some people. However, in particular the small industrial pistols are very suitable for fast creation of even basecoats on human bodies. The handling of the lacquer pistols is very easy thanks to their control trigger, and they spray large amounts of paint within a short time thanks to their large nozzles (in part more than 1 mm).

AIRBRUSHES

FARBVERSORGUNG

Neben der Bedienbarkeit der Geräte ist die Farbzufuhr ein weiteres Unterscheidungskriterium von Airbrushgeräten:

Saugsysteme

Bei sogenannten Saugsystemen wird ein Farbbehälter unter das Gerät gesteckt. Je nach Modell lassen sich entweder direkt die Farbflaschen bestimmter Hersteller anstecken oder die Farbe muss in eigens dafür vorgesehene Plastik-, Glas- oder Metallbehälter umgefüllt werden. Dieser Gerätetyp wird immer dann benutzt, wenn viel Farbe verarbeitet werden soll – ist also ideal für Ganzkörper-Bodypaintings oder auch für Airbrush-Tattoos bei großen Events. Oftmals werden Saugsysteme auch mit großen Düsen- und/oder Single Action-Systemen kombiniert, um schnell und einfach viel Farbe zu transportieren.

Fließsysteme

Für kleinere Farbflächen und detaillierte Designs wie z.B. einzelne Tattoos, Nail Art, Make-Up, Haargestaltung oder Facepainting reicht ein kleinerer Becher, der oben auf dem Gerät angebracht ist. Solche Modelle nennt man Fließsysteme, da die Farbe vom Farbbecher oder einer Farbmulde aus in das Gerät hineinfließt. Einige Hersteller liefern diese Geräte auch mit Deckeln für den Farbbecher aus, was vor allem bei hektischen Einsätzen auf Messen und Events durchaus von Vorteil sein kann, um Flecken zu vermeiden.

Seitenanschlusssysteme

Eher exotisch sind dagegen Seitenanschlusssysteme, die sich je nach Bedarf von Fließ- auf Saugsystem umrüsten lassen. Diese Geräte sind in der Regel 20-40 Euro teurer und werden von nur wenigen Herstellern angeboten. So ein System ist sicherlich durchaus praktisch und eine preisgünstige Einstiegsvariante, wenn beides gewünscht wird. Allerdings sind diese Geräte konstruktionsbedingt sehr seitenlastig und damit für viele Airbrusher gewöhnungsbedürftig.

PAINT FEED

Besides the handling of the devices, the paint feed is another distinct characteristic of the airbrush devices:

Bottom-Feed

For bottom-feed, a colour cup is mounted underneath the device. Depending on the model, the paint bottles from some manufacturers can be used directly or the paint must be poured into a special plastic, glass or metal container. This type of paint feed is best suitable when a lot of paint is needed – it is ideal for whole body paintings, airbrush tanning as well as for airbrush tattoos a performed at large events. Often, the bottom-feed system is combined with large nozzle and/or single-action systems to allow for quick and simple transport of large paint volumes.

Gravity-Feed

For smaller paint areas and detailed designs such as individual tattoos, nail art, make-up, hair art or face painting, a much smaller colour cup is sufficient which is mounted on the top of device. This system is called the gravity-feed because the paint is drawn into the airbrush by simply flowing in. Some manufacturers will enclose a lid for the colour cup in the delivery which is definitely an advantage especially on fast-paced missions at trade fairs and events to prevent stains.

Side-Feed

The somewhat exotic side-feed system can be converted into a bottom-feed or gravity-feed system according to the actual need. These devices usually cost 20-40 € more and only a few manufacturers produce them. Such a system is definitely convenient and a reasonably priced alternative for beginners if they wish both of the systems. However, with the load placed on the side, these devices take some getting use to for many airbrushers.

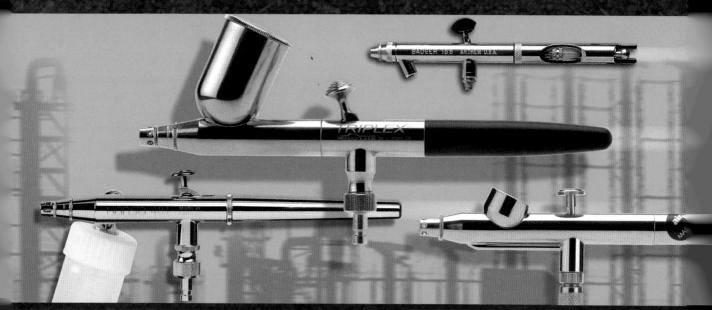

DÜSENSYSTEME UND -GRÖSSEN

Düse und Nadel sind die Herzstücke eines Airbrushgerätes. Sind diese nicht in Ordnung, kann das Gerät nicht richtig funktionieren. Ergebnis: Das Spritzbild ist unsauber, der Farbauftrag ungleichmäßig. Bei den Düsen unterscheidet man Steck- und Schraubdüsen. Beide Typen haben ihre Vor- und Nachteile. Schraubdüsen können nur unter Zuhilfenahme eines kleinen Schraubschlüssels ausgebaut werden, was bei jeder gründlichen Reinigung des Gerätes notwendig ist. Dreht man bei diesem filigranen Bauteil unter Umständen in die falsche Richtung, kann das Gewinde brechen. Ihr Vorteil ist jedoch, dass die Schraubdüse im Gegensatz zur Steckdüse direkt mit dem Geräte-Gehäuse verbunden ist und es so seltener zu Problemen mit der Luftabdichtung kommt.

Die Steckdüsen lassen sich dagegen sehr schnell und einfach austauschen. Allerdings muss hier öfter die Dichtung überprüft und ausgetauscht werden. Kommt diese Düsendichtung dann mal abhanden, ist das Gerät quasi lahmgelegt.

Je nach Farbmenge und Konsistenz der Farbe kann man verschiedene Düsengrößen für das Airbrushgerät auswählen. Zur Auswahl stehen je nach Hersteller etwa Düsengrößen zwischen 0,15 und 1,0 mm Durchmesser. Bei einigen Herstellern ist die Düse (Schraubdüsensysteme) direkt mit dem Gerät verbunden und kann nur mit einer Düsengröße verwendet werden. Dementsprechend braucht man dann mehrere Geräte, wenn man mit verschiedenen Düsengrößen arbeiten möchte. Bei anderen Herstellern lassen sich aber auch verschiedene Düsengrößen (Steckdüsen) in ein Gerät einsetzen, so dass man je nach Anwendung flexibel wechseln kann. Mit dem Wechsel der Düsengröße wird bei den meisten Geräten darüber hinaus immer auch der Austausch der Nadel und des Luftkopfes notwendig.

Das Vorurteil, nur mit feinen Düsen ließe sich ein feines Spritzbild erzeugen, hält sich – vor allem dank der Hersteller und Händler, die möglichst viele Teile verkaufen möchten – hartnäckig. Vielmehr ist das eine Frage des Könnens: Wer das Gerät beherrscht, kann auch mit größeren Düsen sehr fein sprühen. Kleine Düsengrößen wie 0,15 mm sind für Bodypainting überhaupt nicht geeignet, da Bodypaintings selten so detailliert sind und auch die Farbe meist eine größere Düse verlangt. Ab einer Düsengröße von 0,2 mm (je nach Farbe) ist man da schon besser bedient. Für Ganzkörperbodypainting eignen sich Düsengrößen von 0,4 bis 1,0 mm.

NOZZLE SYSTEMS AND SIZES

The nozzle and the needle are the heart of any airbrush device. The device cannot work properly without them being in the right place. Result: The spray pattern is not clean, the paint is applied unevenly. There are quick-change and screw-in nozzles both of which have their pros and cons. The screw-in nozzle systems can only be removed with the help of a little screw wrench and removing these nozzles is necessary for solid cleaning. When you screw this fragile component into the wrong direction, you can occasionally "screw it up", and the thread will break. However, the advantage is that screw-in nozzles – opposed to the quick-change nozzles – are directly connected to the body of the device and due to this fact there are less problems with the air seal.

On the contrary, the quick-change nozzle can be swapped very quickly. However, the sealing must be checked and replaced more often too. If this nozzle seal ever goes missing, the whole device is paralyzed.

Depending on the amount of pain and its consistency, there are various nozzle sizes available for airbrush devices. Depending on the manufacturer, there are nozzle sizes with a diameter ranging from 0,15 mm to 1,0 mm. The nozzles of the devices supplied by some manufacturers (screw-in systems) are directly connected to the device and can only be used with the one particular nozzle size. According to this, more devices are necessary to work with different nozzle sizes. Other manufacturers offer devices which can work with various nozzle sizes (quick-change systems) allowing for more flexibility as the user can swap the nozzle according to the application. For most of the devices available, swapping the nozzle size will always imply swapping the needle and the air head.

The prejudice, that only with fine nozzles it is possible to create a finely spray pattern, has been very persistent – in particular thanks to the manufacturers and trade people who want to sell as many devices as possible. Much more though, it is a question of your competence and mastery: If you have mastered a device, you can work with larger nozzles and still create a very fine pattern. Small nozzle sizes such as 0,15 mm are not suitable for body painting at all because body paintings are only rarely rich in detail, and also the paint requires a larger nozzle. Depending on paint, bodypainters are better served with 0,2 mm nozzles and bigger. For the whole body painting, nozzle sizes between 0,4 mm and 1,0 mm are even better suitable.

TIPPS ZUM AIRBRUSH-KAUF

Bei der Wahl eines Airbrushgerätes kommt es also auf unterschiedliche Faktoren an. Farbmenge, Größe des Paintings, gewünschte Handhabung und das Düsensystem entscheiden darüber, welches Gerät für Sie persönlich ideal ist. Beim Kauf eines Airbrushgerätes sollten Sie darüber hinaus auch noch auf die Preise und Verfügbarkeit der Ersatzteile sowie den damit verbundenen Wartungsaufwand achten. Sicherlich ist es wünschenswert, dass Sie als Einsteiger z.B. die Möglichkeit haben, unterschiedliche Geräte zu testen. Diese Möglichkeiten gibt es gelegentlich in einem Fachgeschäft, vor allem aber bieten Airbrushkurse oder Messen die Gelegenheit, sich mit den unterschiedlichen Marken und Herstellern vertraut zu machen.

TIPS FOR AIRBRUSH SHOPPING

So, while choosing an airbrush device, it is important to respec different characteristics. Paint amount, size of the body painting desired handling and the nozzle system rule the decision which device is the best one for you personally. While buying an airbrush device, you should also pay attention to the price and to the availability of spare parts as well as the required maintenance effort. I is certainly desirable to be able to test different devices if you are a beginner. On occasion, you may "get lucky" in a specialized shop but above all, airbrush courses and trade fairs offer you the opportunity to make yourself familiar with the various brands anc manufacturers.

There are airbrush devices in all quality and price ranges A good airbrush device is available from ca 100 €. Certainly, the paint is also going to come out of the cheap Asian merchandise which can be purchased on eBay. However, the question if the device will be working well and if spare parts are available some times remains open.

Airbrushgeräte gibt es in verschiedenen Güte- und Preisklassen: Ein gutes Airbrushgerät bekommen Sie ab ca. 100 Euro. Asiatische Billiggeräte, die oftmals bei Ebay gehandelt werden, können sicherlich auch Farbe versprühen. Ob das Gerät aber wirklich gut funktioniert und auch noch eine Ersatzteilversorgung sichergestellt werden kann, ist dabei eher fraglich.

DIE LUFTQUELLE
AIR SOURCES

WENN MAN SICH die kunstvollen Airbrush-Arbeiten ansieht, glauben viele, dass es beim Werkzeug nur auf die richtige Spritzpistole und Farbe ankommt. Nicht zu vergessen ist aber die – meist unterm Tisch versteckte – Luftquelle, die der Technik überhaupt erst ihren Namen und Eigenschaften gibt.

MANY WHO LOOK at the cunning airbrush works believe that it is only conditioned by the use of the following tools – the spray pistol and the paints. However, the air source – mostly hidden under the table – must not be forgotten because this is where the name and the characteristics of this technique originate.

Prinzipiell gibt es viele Möglichkeiten, das Airbrushgerät mit Luft zu versorgen: Von der Druckluftflasche über Autoreifen und Baukompressoren bis hin zu Öl-Kolbenkompressoren. In der Praxis haben sich letztendlich jedoch spezielle Airbrushkompressoren – Membran-, ölgeschmierte und öllose Kolbenkompressoren – durchgesetzt.

Die Unterschiede zwischen den Kompressoren liegen im Wesentlichen in der Leistung, im Gewicht, der Lautstärke und im Preis. Für einen Anfänger sind die Anschaffungskosten eines Kompressors nicht unerheblich, denn ein Kompressor kann ohne weiteres mehr kosten als der Rest der Airbrushausrüstung zusammen. Deshalb kommt es oft zu einem Kompromiss zwischen dem, was man eigentlich braucht und wieviel man auszugeben bereit ist. Die langlebigen und leistungsfähigen Kompressoren kosten naturgemäß am meisten.

Das Gewicht und die Lautstärke eines Kompressors bestimmen die Wahl vor allem dann, wenn man das Gerät z.B. in einem Geschäft oder Studio einsetzt oder es häufig transportieren muss, z.B. bei Event-Einsätzen. So gibt es z.B. leistungsstarke, kaum hörbare Silent-Air Kompressoren, die aber mindestens 17 kg wiegen. Bei kleinen kompakten Kompressoren muss man dagegen eher Leistungseinbußen (zumindest im Hinblick auf umfangreiche Ganzkörperbodypaintings) sowie ein hörbares Rattern in Kauf nehmen.

Generell empfiehlt es sich aber, auch als Anfänger nicht am Kompressor zu sparen. Gerade am Anfang weiß man ja nicht unbedingt, auf welche Dinge man als Airbrusher zukünftig vorbereitet sein muss. Eine wirklich zuverlässige Luftquelle kann dabei viel Ärger ersparen – vor allem, wenn Airbrush nicht nur als Hobby, sondern auch beruflich eingesetzt wird und der Job u.a. von der richtigen Funktion der Ausrüstung abhängt.

On principle, there are many possibilities how air can be provided for the airbrush device: Ranging from the propellent cans, car tyres and building sites compressors to oil-operated piston compressors. However, based on practical experience special airbrush compressors have won most recognition – membrane, oil-operated and oil-less piston compressors.

The differences between the compressors are most notable in suction power, weight, sound level and price. For a beginner, the acquisition costs of a compressor are not negligible as a compressor can cost more than the rest of the airbrush equipment all together. Therefore, the final decision is often a compromise between what is actually needed and how much should be spent on it. Naturally, the durable and high-capacity compressors are the most expensive.

The weight and the sound level of a compressor are the most important factors affecting the choice especially when most of the work takes place for example in a shop or a studio, or when the compressor must be carried around a lot such as in the case of events. There are e.g. powerful, scarcely audible Silent-Air compressors, however, these weigh at least 17 kg. In the case of the smaller compressors, there are usually some efficiency losses (at least as far as the whole body painting is concerned) and audible chattering.

In general, beginners are not well advised if they try to save money when buying a compressor. In particular in the beginning, it is not clear what kind of future should be anticipated by the airbrusher and what he needs to be ready for. A truly reliable air source can help to avoid a lot of anger – especially if the art of airbrush is not meant to be only a hobby but also a profession where the job certainly – among other things – depends on the well functioning equipment.

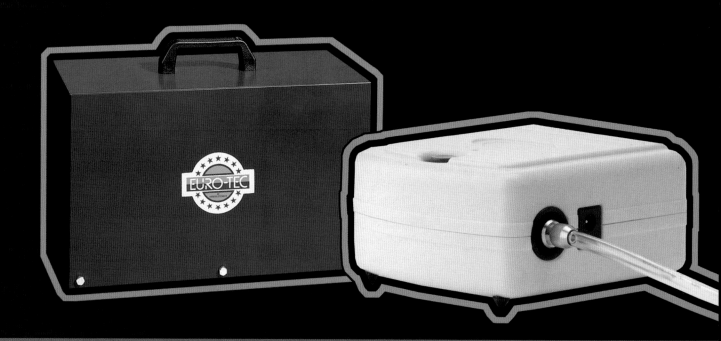

MEMBRANKOMPRESSOREN

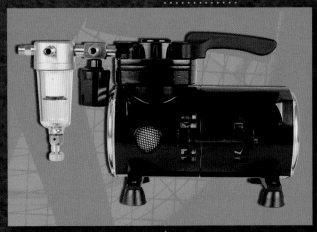

Zum Einstieg in die Technik sind preiswerte Membrankompressoren beliebt (Preisbereich bis 250 Euro). Die Lufterzeugung bei den Membrankompressoren geschieht durch eine Welle, die eine Membrane bewegt und dadurch im Zylinder Druckluft bereitstellt, die durchaus für die meisten Einsatzgebiete ausreichend ist. Eine einfache und effiziente Mechanik, die mit einigen wenigen Bauteilen auskommt und deshalb meist klein und leicht ist. Sofern man sich an die Anweisungen in der Bedienungsanleitung des Herstellers hält, in der regelmäßige Pausen zum Abkühlen des Gerätes vorgeschrieben sind, erreichen Membrankompressoren eine lange Lebensdauer.

Ein Nachteil ist jedoch ihre Lautstärke, die sich nicht unbedingt nur in der angegebenen Dezibel-Zahl ausdrückt, sondern vielmehr in der von Ihnen individuell empfundenen Geräuschkulisse. Auch ein leises Surren, Rattern oder Rasseln kann auf Dauer nervtötend sein. Einige Geräte vibrieren auch und manche haben sogar die Tendenz, sich hin- und her zu bewegen, sobald sie eingeschaltet sind.

Werden all diese Dinge berücksichtigt, kann ein Membrankompressor im individuellen Fall durchaus das richtige Gerät für den Einstieg und den mobilen Einsatz sein. Selbst wenn man später einmal feststellt, dass die Leistung auf Dauer nicht mehr ausreicht, wird man ihn für einige spezielle Anlässe noch gerne benutzen. Membrankompressoren lassen sich hauptsächlich für Make-Up, Airbrush-Tattoos und Facepainting einsetzen.

MEMBRANE COMPRESSORS

The reasonably priced membrane compressors are popular as an introduction into the technique (the price is under 250 €). In the membrane compressor the air production happens via a wave which moves the membrane and so provides pressurized air for the cylinder, and which definitely is sufficient for the most application fields. This simple and efficient mechanism works with only a few components and is therefore small and lightweight. As long as due respect is paid to the manufacturer´s manual prescribing that the compressor must be allowed to cool down in regular intervals, the membrane compressor can prove to be very durable.

One of their disadvantages is the sound level which is not necessarily expressed only through the decibel count but much more through the background noise which you personally perceive. Even a silent buzzing, chattering or rattling can be very annoying when it lasts for some time. Some devices vibrate and some even tend to move from one spot to another as soon as they are switched on.

If the due respect is paid to all these things, the membrane compressor can absolutely be the right device for the introduction and the mobil use. Even if you later find out that the productive capacity is not sufficient anymore, you will still be gladly using it on special occasions. Membrane compressors are best suitable mainly for make-up, airbrush tattoos and face painting.

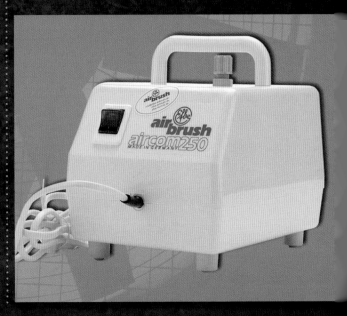

KOLBENKOMPRESSOREN

Vor allem unter Profis verbreiteter sind ölgeschmierte oder öllose Kolbenkompressoren. Diese verfügen über einen Kolben – ähnlich dem eines Automotors. Mit dessen Hilfe wird die Luft komprimiert. Diese Kompressortypen sind erheblich effizienter als Membrankompressoren, extrem leise und leistungsstark, aber auch etwas teurer. Der Geräuschpegel sowie im Übrigen auch die Bauweise entspricht dem eines Kühlschrank-Verdichters. Je nach Modell lässt sich sogar mit mehreren Airbrushgeräten gleichzeitig arbeiten.

Kleine moderne Kolbenkompressoren arbeiten heutzutage öllos. Dies wird durch neue synthetische Schmiermittel ermöglicht, die bereits während der Fertigung eingebracht werden und ein ganzes Kompressorleben lang halten. Öllose Kolbenkompressoren sind sowohl in Gewicht und Größe als auch im Preis eine gute Alternative zu Membrankompressoren. Sie sind absolut wartungsfrei und liegen im Geräuschpegel zwischen Membran- und Öl-Kolbenkompressoren.

Wer den professionellen Weg gehen möchte, überwiegend an einem Ort, häufig und lange arbeitet und ggf. sogar mit mehreren Airbrushgeräten gleichzeitig sprühen möchte, greift zum Öl-Kolbenkompressor. Diese Geräte sind sehr leise und müssen bei Inbetriebnahme lediglich mit dem beiliegenden Öl versorgt werden. Ein Wiederauffüllen des Öls ist nur selten notwendig. Große Öl-Kolbenkompressoren verfügen darüber hinaus in der Regel über einen Lufttank, der Druckluft über einen längeren Zeitraum vorhält. Dadurch produziert der Kompressor nur solange Luft, bis der Luftdruck im Tank eine bestimmte Höhe erreicht hat, und schaltet sich dann automatisch ab. Dies trägt zur längeren Lebensdauer des Kompressors bei und ermöglicht eine Luftversorgung mit konstantem Druck.

Öl-Kolbenkompressoren und leistungsstarke öllose Kolbenkompressoren sind ideal für ein Ganzkörper-Airbrush und Airbrush-Nail Art.

PISTON COMPRESSORS

The oil-operated as well as the oil-less piston compressors are very popular especially amongst professionals. These compressors have a piston that is similar to the one in an automotive engine. With the help of this piston, the air is compressed. This compressor type is considerably more efficient than the membrane compressors, extremely quiet and powerful, but also somewhat more expensive. The sound level as well as the construction correspond with the compressor of a refrigerator. Depending on the model, it is even possible to work with more than one airbrush device at the same time.

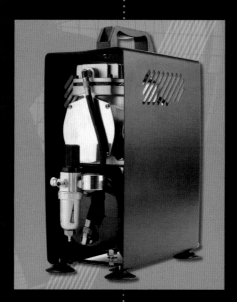

Nowadays, the small, modern piston compressors operate without oil. This is possible thanks to the new synthetic lubricants which are inserted already in the production stage and last for the whole of the compressor´s lifetime. When compared to the weight, size and price of the membrane compressors, oil-less piston compressors present a good alternative. They require no maintenance and their sound level is somewhere between the membrane and the oil-operated piston compressors.

If you want to take the professional path, work often, long and mostly on one spot, or even with more than one airbrush device at once, you will go for the oil-operated piston compressor. These devices are very quiet and must be only oiled with the enclosed oil before initiation. It is seldom necessary to repeatedly add oil. In addition, large oil-operated piston compressors usually have an air tank which preserves air pressure for a longer period of working time. Thus, the compressor only produces air until the air pressure in the air tank reaches a certain level, and then shuts off automatically. This contributes to a longer lifetime of the compressor and allows for an air source with a constant pressure.

Oil-operated piston compressors and powerful oil-less piston compressors are ideal for whole body airbrush and for the airbrush nail art.

SONDERKOMPRESSOREN

Neben den schon aufgeführten Kompressorentypen gibt es speziell für den mobilen Make-up-Einsatz auch ganz kleine Kompressoren. Diese sind nicht so leistungsstark, aber reichen gerade aus, um einen zarten Farbhauch im Gesicht aufzutragen. Einige Modelle können sogar mit Batterien betrieben werden.

Achten Sie bei diesen Geräten aber darauf, dass evtl. ein zusätzlicher Kondenswasserfilter am Airbrushgerät montiert werden sollte, da sonst recht schnell Kondenswasser im Schlauch entsteht und auf das Gesicht gespritzt wird. Auch bei der geringeren Benutzungsdauer sollten Pausen eingehalten werden, damit das Gerät nicht überhitzt wird.

SPECIAL COMPRESSORS

Beside the above listed types of compressors, there are also special small compressors for the mobil make-up work. They are not so powerful but still sufficient for the application of a fine paint layer on the face. Some of the models can even work battery-operated.

While looking at these devices, special attention needs to be paid to the possible need of an additional condensate filter which should be installed on the airbrush device so that there is no condensed water in the air line which could end up on the face. Even if the time of use is not long, the intervals for cooling down should be respected so that the device does not overheat.

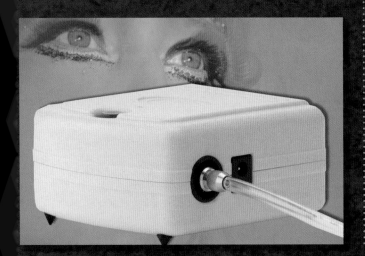

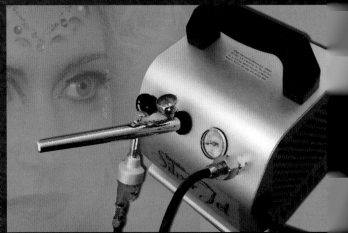

WEITERE TIPPS ZUM KOMPRESSOR-KAUF

Jeder Kompressor, egal welcher Bauart, sollte

▶ über einen Druckminderer verfügen, um den Druck je nach Farbe und Anwendung justieren zu können,

▶ einen Wasserabscheider haben, damit das Kondenswasser gesammelt wird und sich nicht mit der versprühten Luft mischt,

▶ eine Abschaltautomatik (im Modellnamen oft durch A oder AS gekennzeichnet) enthalten, damit der Kompressor zur Ruhe kommt, wenn keine Luft benötigt wird. Dies ist energiesparend und schont den Kompressor.

Auf der Suche nach einem Kolbenkompressor stoßen Sie sicherlich bei einigen Händlern auf ähnliche Produktbezeichnungen wie z.B. Silentair 20a, Euro-Tec 20a, HANSA HTC20A. Alle diese Kompressoren kommen vom gleichen Hersteller und unterscheiden sich nur in wenigen Details wie Farbe und kleineren bautechnischen Veränderungen.

TIPS FOR COMPRESSOR SHOPPING

Every compressor, no matter what its construction is, should

▶ have a pressure reducer to allow for controlling the pressure depending on paint and application type;

▶ have a water separator which collects the condensed water and prevents it from mixing with the air;

▶ have an automatic shut-off (often indicated as A or AS within the model name) so that the compressor can rest when there is no need to produce air. This is energy efficient and protects the compressor from damage.

When looking for a piston compressor, you will probably run into similar product names such as Silentair 20a, Euro-Tec 20a, HANSA HTC20A in many shops. All these compressors come from the same manufacturer and vary only in small detail such as colour and minor modifications of construction.

KOMPRESSOREN

INBETRIEBNAHME ÖLLOSER KOMPRESSOR

Beispiel: Euro-Tec 10a

Die Inbetriebnahme dieses öllosen Kolbenkompressors ist ganz einfach.

1. Zuerst verschraubt man den schwarzen Schlauch zwischen Wasserabscheider und Druckschalter.

2. Als nächstes wird der Airbrushanschluss an den Wasserabscheider geschraubt.

INITIATION OIL-LESS COMPRESSOR

Example: Euro-Tec 10a

The initiation of this oil-less compressor is very easy:

1. First, screw the black hose to the water separator and to the pressure switch.

2. Then, screw the junction to the water separator.

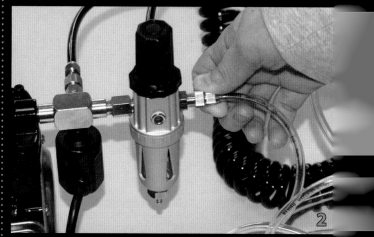

3. Am Ende des Schlauches ist eine Schnellkupplung angebracht, mit der das Airbrushgerät schnell und vor allem komfortabel verbunden werden kann. Einfach das Gerät darauf stecken und ruck zuck ist die Verbindung hergestellt.

4. Der Kompressor wird an eine Stromquelle angeschlossen und mit dem an der Seite angebrachten Schalter eingeschaltet.

3. At the end of the hose, there is a quick coupler allowing for a quick and especially comfortable connection to the airbrush device. Simply plug the device in and the connection is set up in no time.

4. Plug the compressor into a power source and switch it on with the button on its side.

5. Den Druck regulieren Sie, indem Sie zunächst den Dreh-knopf nach oben ziehen.

6. Um den Druck zu erhöhen, drehen Sie den Drehknopf im Uhrzeigersinn.

5. You can control the pressure through pulling up the rotary knob.

6. Turn the knob in the clockwise direction to increase the pressure.

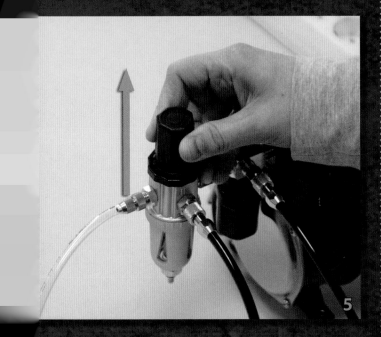

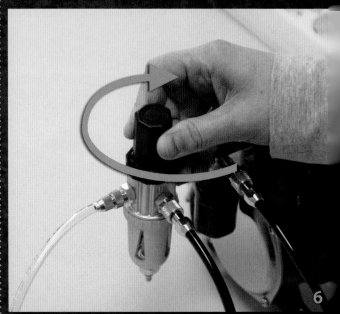

7. Möchten Sie den Druck vermindern, um z.B. Farbe oder Make-up im Gesicht aufzutragen, dann drehen Sie den Knopf gegen den Uhrzeigersinn. Ist der gewünschte Arbeitsdruck eingestellt, drücken Sie den Drehknopf wieder nach unten.

8. Um das Kondenswasser aus dem Wasserabscheider zu las-sen, drücken Sie den Ablass-Hebel unter dem Wasserab-scheider mit dem Finger nach oben, bis das Wasser vollstän-dig entwichen ist. Wenn Sie den Ablass-Hebel wieder loslas-sen, schließt er automatisch.

7. To reduce the pressure, e.g. for applying paint or make-up in the face, turn the knob in the anti clockwise direction. Having reached the desired pressure, press the knob down again.

8. To let the condensate out of the water separator, push up the lever underneath the water separator with your finger until all the water is gone. When you let go on the lever, it automati-cally shuts off.

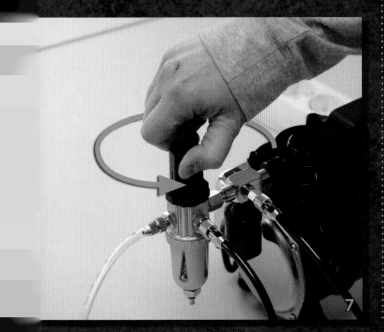

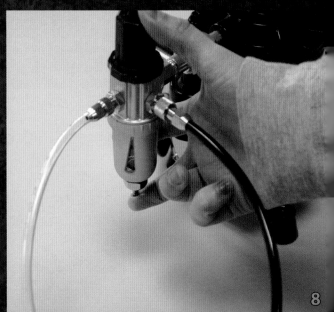

INBETRIEBNAHME
ÖL-KOLBENKOMPRESSOR

Beispiel: Sil Air 20a

Die erste Inbetriebnahme eines Öl-Kolbenkompressors ist ebenfalls recht einfach und schnell vorzunehmen. Je nach Hersteller werden unterschiedliche Anschlussmöglichkeiten für den Kompressor schon mitgeliefert. In der Regel muss aber noch das Öl eingefüllt und der Filter aufgesteckt werden, bevor der Kompressor an die Stromquelle angeschlossen werden kann.

1. Entfernen Sie die Transportsicherung aus Pappe. Einfach herausziehen.

2. Ziehen Sie den Öl-Einfüllstöpsel ab und bewahren Sie diesen für evtl. spätere Transporte auf.

3. Entnehmen Sie das Zubehör aus der Plastiktüte. Je nach Anbieter finden Sie unterschiedliche Teile vor. In diesem Fall: Luftfilter, Einfülltülle für die Ölflasche, Schnellkupplung, Stecknippel, Doppelnippel (wird aber meistens nicht benötigt).

4. Schneiden Sie die Öffnung der Einfülltülle mit einem Cutter oder einer Schere oben ab. Öffnen Sie die Ölflasche und entfernen Sie die Schutzfolie. Dann können Sie die Einfülltülle auf die Ölflasche schrauben.

5. Kontrollieren Sie, ob der Kompressor ausgeschaltet ist. Schließen Sie dann den Kompressor ans Stromnetz an.

INITIATION
OIL-OPERATED PISTON COMPRESSOR

Example: Sil Air 20a

The initiation of an oil-operated piston compressor is also quite simple and quick. Depending on the manufacturer, there are different connection accessories delivered with the compressor. However, usually you will have to pour in the oil and insert the filter before the compressor can be attached to a power source.

1. Remove the transportation safety board. Simply pull it out.

2. Pull out the plug to pour in the oil and save it for possible transport later on.

3. Take the accessories out of the plastic bag. Depending on the supplier, you will find different parts. In this case: air filter, a nozzle for the oil bottle, quick coupling, plug nipple, double nipple (which is mostly not necessary).

4. Cut off the opening at the head of the nozzle with a cutter or scissors. Open the oil bottle and remove the protection film. Now you can screw the nozzle onto the oil bottle.

5. Check if the compressor is switched off. Then, attach the compressor to a power supply network.

6. Füllen Sie nun das Öl in den Einfüllstutzen am Kompressor. In der Regel müssen Sie die komplette Flasche einfüllen. Lesen Sie hier nochmal genau in der Bedienungsanleitung des Herstellers. Damit das Öl schnell eingefüllt werden kann, haben Sie auch die Möglichkeit, den Kompressor beim Einfüllen einzuschalten. Der Kompressor saugt dann das Öl aus der Flasche heraus.

7. Schalten Sie den Kompressor wieder aus und überprüfen nach einigen Minuten die Füllhöhe. Evtl. können Sie dann den Ölstand noch korrigieren.

6. Pour now the oil into the filler neck on the compressor. Usually, you must pour in the whole bottle. To be sure, read the manufacturer´s instruction manual again. To be able to pour the oil in quickly, you can also switch the compressor on. I will suck the oil out of the bottle.

7. Switch the compressor off again and check the filling leve. after some minutes. Potentially, you might still be able to adjust it.

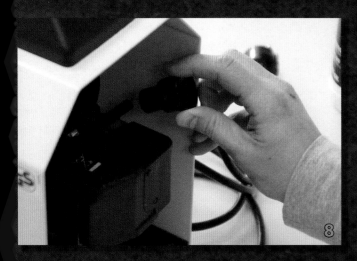

8. Stecken Sie die Luftfilter auf den Einfüllstutzen.

9. Haben Sie ein Gerät, bei dem die Schnellkupplung noch nicht installiert ist, wickeln Sie das beiliegende Teflonband um das Gewinde. Das Teflonband sorgt dafür, dass die Verbindung absolut luftdicht ist.

8. Insert the air filter into the filler neck.

9. If you have a device without a pre-installed quick coupling wrap the enclosed Teflon strap around the thread. This Teflor strap will ensure that the connection will remain absolutely hermetically sealed.

KOMPRESSOREN

10. Schrauben Sie dann die Schnellkupplung in den Kompressor. Nun können Sie einen Schlauch anschließen und den Kompressor wieder einschalten. Achten Sie darauf, dass keine Luft an den Kupplungen entweicht. Sie merken das entweder an einem Zischgeräusch oder wenn der Arbeitsdruck (später abzulesen an der Druckanzeige) absinkt. Falls das der Fall ist, überprüfen Sie nochmal die Abdichtungen und Gewinde.

11. Stellen Sie dann den gewünschten Arbeitsdruck (in der Abbildung 2 bar) ein, indem Sie den Knopf nach oben ziehen und im Uhrzeigersinn drehen, bis der gewünscht Druck angezeigt wird. Idealerweise schließen Sie ein Airbrushgerät beim Einstellen des Arbeitsdrucks an und betätigen den Hebel dabei. Nur so sehen Sie den tatsächlich eingestellten Arbeitsdruck, der sonst um ca. 0,2 bar variieren kann.

10. Then, screw the quick coupling onto the compressor. You can now attach a hose and switch the compressor on. Mind the couplings so that no air comes out. This happenes if you hear a fizzling sound or if the work pressure drops (later displayed on the pressure gauge). If this happens, check the sealings and the threads again.

11. Then, set up the desired working pressure (on the picture 2 bar) through pulling up the knob and turning it in the clockwise direction until the desired pressure is displayed. It is ideal to attach an airbrush device before setting up the working pressure while moving the lever because this way you can see the effective working pressure which can otherwise vary by 0,2 bar.

TIPPS FÜR EIN LANGES KOMPRESSOR-LEBEN

Wenn Sie Ihren Kompressor transportieren möchten, sollte dies im stehenden Zustand vorgenommen werden, damit kein Öl ausläuft. Gerade beim Transport im Auto ist es wichtig, dass dieser nicht umfällt und gut fixiert wird. Als zusätzlichen Schutz können Sie den Luftfilter gegen den Öl-Einfüllstöpsel tauschen. Achten Sie dann aber bei Inbetriebnahme darauf, dass dieser wieder durch den Filter ersetzt wird, da der Kompressor sonst keine Luft ziehen kann und nicht anspringt.

Wurde der Kompressor an einem langen Arbeitstag gut beansprucht, überprüfen Sie, ob sich ein Kondenswasser-Ölgemisch im Lufttank befindet. Schrauben Sie dazu das Ablass-Ventil ein wenig auf und lassen Sie das Gemisch heraus. So stellen Sie sicher, dass nichts durchrostet und Sie über die Jahre ein funktionstüchtiges und zuverlässiges Gerät haben.

Wie auch bei dem öllosen Kompressor können Sie Kondenswasser am Kondenswasserabscheider bei Bedarf entleeren. Dazu einfach das Ventil drehen und nach oben drücken. Nach Ablassen der Flüssigkeit wieder zudrehen.

TIPS FOR A LONG COMPRESSOR LIFE

When you want to transport your compressor, it should always stand on its feet so that no oil can escape. Especially while transporting the compressor in the car it is important to fasten the compressor properly so that it cannot keel over. You can also swap the air filter for the plug. If you do this, remember swapping the plug back for the air filter before switching the compressor on or it will not be able to suck in any air and will not start up.

Has the compressor been drawn on duty for a long working day, check if there is a condensate-oil mix in the tank. To do this, unscrew the drain valve a little and let the mix out. This is how you make sure that nothing will rust so that you can use a still fully functional and reliable device for years.

Same as for the oil-less compressors, you can let the condensed water out with the water separator strainer. To do this simply unscrew the valve and push it up. After the liquid has come out, close the valve again.

FARBEN
PAINTS

GRUNDSÄTZLICH kann mit einem Airbrushgerät alles versprüht werden, was eine flüssige oder milchige Konsistenz hat. Im Handel gibt es spezielle Airbrush-Farben, die sich auf Karton, künstliche Fingernägel oder Metall sprühen lassen, aber nicht für die Haut geeignet sind. Hautfarben unterliegen natürlich strengeren Kriterien hinsichtlich der Hautverträglich-keit und chemischen Zusammensetzung, damit keine Allergien entstehen. Der Hersteller liefert auf Wunsch ein Datenblatt der Inhaltsstoffe. Körperfarben aus den

PRINCIPALLY, an airbrush device can be used to spray eve-rything of a liquid or milky consistency. In trade, there are special airbrush paints that can be sprayed on card-board, artificial nails or metal, but those are not suitab-le for the skin. Skin paints of course underlie very strict criteria of skin friendliness and chemical composition so that no allergies occur. The manufacturers provide a data list of ingredients at wish. Skin paints from the USA should for example be tested and approved by the FDA (Food and Drug Administration)

Zum Airbrushen eignen sich im Bodypainting- und Schmink-bereich natürlich vor allem Flüssigfarben (im Gegensatz zu festen Farben, die mit dem Pinsel angelöst werden müssen). Viele dieser Farben werden bereits „airbrushfertig" ausgeliefert. Darüber hinaus unterscheidet man Farben auf Wasser- und auf Alkoholbasis. Die Farben sollten dann entsprechend nur mit Wasser bzw. Alkohol (Isoprophylalkohol) verdünnt werden. Entfernen lassen sich die Farben z.T. mit Wasser, andere am besten mit Körperöl.

Ein weiteres Unterscheidungsmerkmal von Körper-farben ist ihre Haltbarkeit: Bodypainting-Farben sind sofort wasserlöslich und nur für den maximal eintägigen Effekt bestimmt. Tattoo-Farben dagegen halten einige Tage – nach Angaben der Hersteller 3-7 Tage, was aber je nach Hauttyp nicht immer der Fall ist. Einen Sonderfall dagegen bilden Tanning-Lotionen: Sie können sowohl sofort einen „gefärbten" Bräunungseffekt erzielen, als auch mit Hilfe von Selbstbräunungs-wirkstoffen eine Hautbräunung hervorrufen.

Die folgende Liste enthält die wichtigsten in Europa erhältlichen Farben für Airbrush-Bodypainting, -Tattoos, -Make-up und -Tanning. Darüber hinaus gibt es zahlreiche Eigen-marken von Händlern und Anbietern, die auf Abfüllungen der genannten Produkte oder auf individuellen Eigenrezepturen beruhen. Diese werden dann oftmals aber nur von der jeweiligen Firma zum Direktverkauf angeboten.

For airbrushing in the body painting and make-up field, liquid paints are naturally the most suitable ones (they don´t need to be dissolved with a paintbrush as it is the case with firm paints). Many colours are already supplied "airbrush-ready". Moreover, there are water-based and alcohol-based paints. According to this, the paints should only be thinned with water or respectively with alcohol (isoprophyl alcohol). Some paints can be removed with water, others with body oil.

Another differentiating factor of body paints is the time they last on the skin: Body painting paints are immediately water soluble and meant to last a maximum of a one-day effect. On the opposite, tattoo paints can last several days – according to the manufacturers´ specifications 3-7 days, which though – depending upon the skin type – is not always the case. Tanning lotions are an exception: they can immediately create a "painted" tan effect, or they can be used to initiate a skin tanning process with the self tanning agents.

The following list contains the most important paints for airbrush body painting, tattoos, make-up and tanning available in Europe. There are also several brands of manufacturers and suppliers which are based on the fillings of the above mentioned products or on individual recipes but are often on offer only by the particular manufacturer and for direct sales.

AIRBRUSH-BODYPAINTING-FARBEN   *AIRBRUSH BODY PAINTING PAINTS*

Diamond FX Liquid Colors

Die flüssigen Airbrush-Make-up-Farben sind erst jüngst mit zehn Bunt- und zwei Metallic-Farbtönen in jeweils 60 ml-Fläschchen in den Handel gestartet. Die Diamond FX-Farbe ist sehr dünnflüssig und ohne Verdünnung oder Zusätze mit einer Düse ab 0,2 mm sprühbar. Sie ist extrem deckend, sehr farbintensiv und ermöglicht ein schnelles und sparsames Arbeiten. Die Farbtöne sind auf das Diamond FX Festfarbensortiment abgestimmt und lassen sich gut damit kombinieren. Die Inhaltsstoffe der Farbe entsprechen den europäischen und internationalen Vorschriften sowie der amerikanischen FDA-Verordnung.

Diamond FX Liquid Colors

Diamond FX have only just started to offer in trade the liquid airbrush make-up paints in 10 coloured and 2 metallic colour tones, each in 60 ml bottle. The Diamond FX airbrush paint is very thin and can be sprayed with 0,2 mm nozzles and bigger without any additionals or thinning. It is extremely opaque and very colour-intensive, and it allows for a fast and economical working. The colour tones of the liquid paints are complementary to the standard colour assortment of Diamond SX and can be therefore very well combined with these. The ingredients of the paints are consistent with European and international legal prescriptions and they have been also approved by the American FDA.

Eulenspiegel Pro-Make-up

Eulenspiegel Pro-Make-up-Farben sind wasserlöslich und müssen immer – am besten mit Mixing-Liquid Flüssigkeit des Herstellers – verdünnt werden. Die Farben werden soweit verdünnt, bis sie einen milchigen Zustand erreichen, und sind dann für Düsengrößen ab 0,2 mm geeignet. Mit Wasser und Seife lässt sich die Farbe schnell wieder entfernen, bei Gelb und Rot als Grundierung müssen mehrere Waschgänge vorgenommen werden. Die Farbe lässt sich mit den trockenen Pro-Make-up Airbrush-Pigmenten auch selber herstellen, die mit Mixing-Liquid angerührt werden. Das Angebot umfasst 23 Farbtöne sowie 6 Perlmutt-Pigmente.

Eulenspiegel Pro-Make-up

Eulenspiegel Pro-Make-Up paints are water soluble and must always be thinned. The manufacturer recommends the Mixing-Liquid as the most suitable. The paints must be thinned to attain a milky consistency. Then, they are suitable for nozzles from 0,2 mm up. The paint can be quickly removed with water and soap. However, if red and yellow are used as a basecoat, several washes are necessary. The paint can also be self made with the Pro-Make-Up Airbrush-Pigments. These are dry pigments which can be stirred with Mixing-Liquid. There are 23 colour tones as well as 6 pearl pigments on offer.

Fardel Fluid Body Paint

Fardel Créations bietet flüssige Bodypainting-Farben an, die sich unverdünnt oder im Verhältnis 1:1 mit Wasser verdünnt mit der Spritzpistole versprühen lassen. Sie zeichnen sich durch eine lange Haltbarkeit am Körper aus, lassen sich aber auch problemlos mit Wasser abwaschen. Alle Farben sind dermatologisch getestet und enthalten keine tierischen Bestandteile. Dank verzögerter Trocknungszeiten lassen sich die Farben auch am Körper gut bearbeiten. Für das Bodypainting stehen 66 Farbtöne zur Verfügung.

Fardel Fluid Body Paint

Fardel Créations offers liquid bodypainting paints which can be used with an airbrush device unthinned or thinned with water at a ratio 1:1. They stand out because of their long lasting preservation on the body but they can still be washed off easily with water. All the paints are dermatologically tested and do not contain any animal component. Thanks to the longer drying period, it is possible to work with these paints also on the body very well. The paints are available in 66 colour tones for bodypainting.

FARBEN

Kryolan Air Stream Make-up Colors

Diese Bodypainting- und Make-up-Farben sind so eingestellt, dass sie sich mit sehr geringem Arbeitsdruck (unter 0,5 bar) sprühen lassen. Die Air Stream Make-up Colors werden aus einer Entfernung von ca. 10 bis 15 cm gesprüht und trocknen schnell und wischfest auf. Die Air Stream Make-up-Farben werden in 24 Farbvarianten ausgeliefert. Zusätzlich stehen 30 weitere Farben für ein umfangreiches Body Make-up zur Verfügung, diese Farben sind in der EU auch für das Gesicht zugelassen.

Kryolan Air Stream Make-up Colors

These body painting and make-up paints are designed for spraying under low working pressure (under 0,5 bar). The Air Stream Make-Up Colors are to be sprayed from a distance of ca 10 to 15 cm, they dry fast and smear-resistant. The Stream Make-Up Colors are available in 24 colour variations. In addition, there are 30 more colours available for an extensive body make-up; within the EU, the use of these paints on the face is permitted.

Mehron Professional Liquid Make-up

Mehron Professional Liquid Make-up ist eine hoch pigmentierte und wasserlösliche Farbe, die ausschließlich aus FDA geprüften Stoffen hergestellt wird. Das Sortiment umfasst 24 Farbtöne für Bodypainting und Make-up. Verdünnt mit einem Mixing Liquid lässt sich die Farbe mit einer Düse ab 0,2 mm versprühen. Die Farbe lässt sich mit Wasser und Seife leicht wieder abwaschen. Das Sortiment bietet auch spezielle Airbrush-Reiniger, Make-up-Entferner sowie Fixier-Sprays.

Mehron Professional Liquid Make-up

Mehron Professional Liquid Make-Up is a highly pigmented and water soluble paint which is manufactured exclusively out of FDA-approved ingredients. The assortment contains 24 colour tones for body painting and make-up. Thinned with a Mixing Liquid, the paint can be sprayed with a 0,2 mm nozzle or bigger. The paint can be easily removed with water and soap. The assortment offers also a special airbrush cleaner, make-up remover as well as spray fixative.

Temptu Dura Airbrush

Temptu Dura Airbrush lassen sich für Airbrush-Bodypainting, -Make-up, -Tattoos und Special Effects verwenden und sind auch unter Studio-Licht lange haltbar und deckend. Das Sortiment unterteilt sich in sechs Ranges: „Original" ist die klassische Bodyart-Linie mit 12 Grund- und Mischtönen. Zehn „Shimmers"-Farbtöne enthalten Mikro-Glitter-Partikel für einen glamourösen Look. „Body Foundations" umfasst 12 Foundation-Hauttöne, „Blacklight" bietet unter Schwarzlicht phosphorisierende Farben. „Specialty" ist für Special Effects konzipiert und umfasst 70 Farbtöne. Das neueste „Platinum"-Sortiment verfügt über eine verlängerte Haltbarkeit von vier bis zehn Tagen und eignet sich besonders für Tattoos.

Temptu Dura Airbrush

Temptu Dura Airbrush can be used for airbrush body painting, make-up, tattoos and special effects. They last long and are very opaque even in the light of a studio. The assortment is divided into six ranges: "Original" is the classical body art line with 12 basic and mixed tones. 10 "Shimmers"-colour tones contain micro-glitter particles for a glamorous look. "Body Foundations" contain 12 foundation skin tones, "Blacklight" offers colours which phosphorise in the black light. The colour series "Speciality" has been designed in particular for special effects and comprises 70 colour tones. The latest "Platinum" assortment stands out with its extended durability from 4 to 10 days, and is therefore most suitable for airbrush tattoos.

AIRBRUSH-TATTOO-FARBEN

AIRBRUSH TATTOO PAINTS

Badger Totally Tattoo

Die Tattoo-Farben von Badger sind auf Alkoholbasis und wasserfest. Sie halten wie bei den meisten Herstellern zwischen 24 und 72 Stunden. Bei der Farbe ist darauf zu achten, dass diese nicht im Gesicht angewendet wird. Vor dem Einsatz muss sie gut aufgeschüttelt werden. Dann eignet sie sich bestens für die Verarbeitung mit der Airbrush. Mit Isopropylalkohol lassen sich die Tattoos leicht wieder entfernen. Totally Tattoo gibt es in 12 verschiedenen Farbtönen.

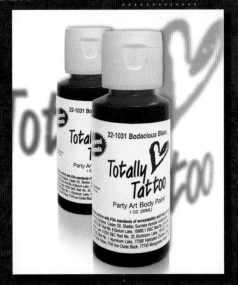

Badger Totally Tattoo

The tattoo paints from Badger are alcohol-based and waterproof. They last between 24 and 72 hours similar to other manufacturers. Make sure that you do not apply these paints on the face. Shake them well before use. Then, they are best suitable for the work with an airbrush. The tattoos can be easily removed with isopropyl alcohol. There are 12 different colour tones of Totally Tattoo.

Eulenspiegel Painted Tattoos

Bei dieser Tattoo-Farbe kann man mit einer Haltbarkeit auf der Haut von bis zu 72 Stunden rechnen. Außerdem kann sie direkt ohne Anmischen aus der Flasche verwendet werden. Bevor man die Farbe nutzt, sollte diese allerdings gut geschüttelt werden, damit sich alle Farbpigmente lösen. Verarbeitbar ist die Farbe mit Düsengrößen ab 0,2 mm. Entfernen lässt sie sich mit Alkohol oder einer Fettcreme. Diese Farbe enthält keinerlei Parfümstoffe oder UV-Filter. Für das Airbrush-Tattoo stehen 14 Farbtöne zur Verfügung.

Eulenspiegel Painted Tattoos

Using this tattoo paint, you can count on its durability on the skin up to 72 hours. What is more, it can be applied directly out of the bottle without mixing. However, before using this paint, shake it well so that all the pigments can dissolve. It is possible to work with this paint with a nozzle size from 0,2 mm. It can be removed with alcohol or with a fat-rich cream. This paint does not contain any perfume substance or filter. For the airbrush tattoos, there are 14 colour tones available.

Mist-Air Body Art Colours

Mist-Air Body Art-Farben sind in 10 Farbtönen erhältlich, die miteinander mischbar sind. Die konzentrierten Farben auf Alkohol-Basis sind sprühfertig, lassen sich sparsam verarbeiten und erzielen eine hohe Farbdichte. Die Farben trocknen auf dem Körper sofort wisch- und wasserfest auf. Mist-Air Tattoos halten etwa zwei bis vier Tage und lassen sich einfach mit Baby-Öl oder Alkohol entfernen. Die Farbinhaltsstoffe entsprechen der FDA-Verordnung.

Mist-Air Body Art Colours

Mist-Air Body Art paints are available in 10 colour tones that can be mixed with each other. The concentrated alcohol-based paints are ready to spray, allow for economical working and provide for a high colour density. The paints dry on the body to immediately become smear-resistant and waterproof. Mist-Air Tattoos last about 2-4 days and can be easily removed with baby oil or alcohol. The paint ingredients are FDA-approved.

Paasche Airbrush Temporary Tattoo

Laut Hersteller halten Paasche Temporary Tattoos durchschnittlich bis zu einer Woche, ab dem fünften Tag verblasst das Motiv in der Regel. Alle Inhaltsstoffe sind von der amerikanischen Behörde FDA zugelassen und wurden unter Laborbedingungen produziert. Das Sortiment umfasst 9 Farbtöne. Der Hersteller empfiehlt zum Versprühen der Farben eine mittlere Düsengröße.

Paasche Airbrush Temporary Tattoo

According to the manufacturer, Paasche Temporary Tattoos can last up to a week time with the motif usually fading from the fifth day on. All ingredients have been approved by the American FDA and were produced under laboratory conditions. The assortment comprises 9 colour tones. For spraying, the manufacturer recommends a middle-sized nozzle.

Senjo-Tattoo

Senjo-Tattoo ist eine tintenähnliche, pigmentfreie Farbe, die sich auch mit feinen 0,15 und 0,2 mm Düsen versprühen lässt. Das Tattoo-Schwarz hat beim Versprühen einen leichten, aber angenehmen Geruch und hinterlässt ein äußerst realistisches Motiv, da die Farbe aus Schwarz, Grün und Blau zusammengesetzt ist. Senjo-Tattoos halten je nach Hauttyp etwa 2-7 Tage. Abgestimmt auf die Farbe ist auch ein Puder zur unsichtbaren Fixierung, ein Hautreiniger sowie ein Airbrush-Cleaner erhältlich.

Senjo-Tattoo

Senjo-Tattoo is an ink-like paint without pigments which can be also sprayed with fine nozzles of 0,15 mm to 0,2 mm. While being sprayed, the tattoo black smells slightly but enjoyably, and it leaves a highly realistic motif because the paint consists of black, green and blue. Senjo-Tattoos last about 2-7 days depending on the skin type. Complementary to the paint, there are a tuned powder for an invisible fixation, a skin cleaner as well as an airbrush cleaner available in trade.

SprayOn Airbrush Tattoo Color

Das Airbrush-Tattoo von SprayOn hält drei bis sieben Tage auf der Haut. Es lässt sich durch fetthaltige Substanzen wieder ablösen. Vor dem Auftragen der Farbe sollte die Haut mit 70% bzw. 100% Isopropylalkohol entfettet werden. Es empfiehlt sich, das fertige Tattoo mit Setting Puder abzupudern. SprayOn bietet 22 Tattoo-Farbtöne an.

SprayOn Airbrush Tattoo Color

The airbrush tattoo from SprayOn lasts on the skin from 3 to 7 days. It can be removed with fat-rich substances. Before application of this paint, the skin should be degreased with a 70% or respectively 100% isopropyl alcohol. It is recommended to finish up the tattoo with Setting Powder. SprayOn offers 22 tattoo colour tones.

MAKE-UP-FARBEN

MAKE-UP PAINTS

Kryolan Aqua Proof

Aqua Proof ist ein mikronisiertes und wasserfestes Make-up in einem alkoholischen Medium zum Aufsprühen mit Airbrush. Aqua Proof wird in einer Auswahl von 24 Haut- und Buntfarben geliefert und kann mit einer Mischung aus MME (Milder Mastix-Entferner) und Hydroöl entfernt werden. Aqua Proof enthält Alkohol und sollte somit nicht in der Nähe der Augen und Schleimhäute angewendet werden.

Kryolan Aqua Proof

Aqua Proof is a micronizing and water-resistant make-up in an alcoholic medium for spraying with an airbrush. Aqua Proof can be delivered in an assortment of 24 skin and pure paints, and can be removed with a mix made out of MME (Mild Spirit Gum Remover) and hydro-oil. Aqua Proof contains alcohol and therefore it should not be used near the eyes and mucosa.

Kryolan Micro Foundation on Air

Dieses Flüssig-Make-up ist speziell für die hochauflösende, digitale Bildtechnik HDTV entwickelt worden. Es wird mit sehr wenig Arbeitsdruck aufgesprüht (höchstens 0,5 bar) und ergibt eine fehlerlose, streifenfreie und gleichmäßige Oberfläche. Micro Foundation on Air trocknet augenblicklich auf und ist anschließend wisch- und abriebfest. Die Foundation lässt sich mühelos mit einem Abschminkmittel entfernen. Sie ist in 36 Farbtönen erhältlich.

Kryolan Micro Foundation on Air

This liquid make-up has been developed especially for the HDTV technique. It shell be sprayed on with only a very low working pressure (maximum of 0,5 bar) and allows for creating an impeccable, stripe-free and even surface. Micro Foundation on Air dries in an instant and is subsequently smear-resistant and abrasion-resistant. The foundation can be removed with a make-up remover at no effort. There are 36 colour tones available.

Mist-Air Professional Airbrush Make-Up

Das Mist Air Airbrush Make-Up Sortiment umfasst 13 Farbtöne auf Silikon- und 13 auf Wasserbasis für Grund- und Augen-Make-up. Außerdem gibt es vier spezielle Rouge-Farben auf Wasserbasis. Alle silikon- bzw. wasserbasierten Farben sind jeweils untereinander mischbar, um Schattierungen und Korrekturen vorzunehmen. Die Farben sind gebrauchsfertig und verfügen laut Hersteller über hervorragende Fließeigenschaften. Die Make-up-Töne auf Silikonbasis lassen sich nicht nur mit Airbrush, sondern auch mit Pinsel und Schwamm gut verarbeiten. Beide Farblinien lassen sich mit einem Make-up-Entferner oder Gesichtsreiniger problemlos entfernen.

Mist-Air Professional Airbrush Make-Up

The Mist-Air Airbrush Make-Up assortment contains 13 silicon-based colour tones and 13 water-based colour tones which can be used to create the base as well as the eye make-up. In addition, there are 4 water-based colour tones to be used specifically for rouge applications. All the silicon-based, respectively water-based paints can be mixed with each other to allow for shadings and corrections of all kind. The paints are ready for use and posses – according to the manufacturer – excellent flow characteristics so that the airbrush device does not clog up. The silicon-based make-up tones can be well handled not only with the airbrush but also with a paintbrush and a sponge. Both paint lines can be removed with a make-up remover or a face cleaner without difficulty.

FARBEN

Mehron New Lux Airbrush Make-up

Das hochpigmentierte New Lux Airbrush Make-up von Mehron basiert auf Wasser und Grünem Tee und wurde mit Vitaminen angereichert. Die spezielle Formel macht das Produkt besonders hautfreundlich und verleiht ihm hohe Deckkraft. New Lux Airbrush Make-up trocknet schnell und bietet ein wasserfestes Finish. Das Präparat ist formaldehyd-, paraben- und halogenfrei und ist mit warmen Wasser und Seife abwaschbar. Mehron bietet diese Serie in 12 Farbtönen an.

Mehron New Lux Airbrush Make-up

The highly pigmented New Lux Airbrush Make-up from Mehron is based on water and green tea, and is fortified with vitamins. The special formula makes the product especially skin friendly and allows for a high opacity. New Lux Airbrush Make-up dries quickly and offers a water-resistant finish. The compound is free of formaldehyde, antihistamine and halogen, and and can be removed with warm water and soap. In this series, Mehron offers 12 colour tones.

SprayOn Airbrush Make-up HD - Aqua Based/Silicone Based

Das Airbrush-Make-up-Sortiment von SprayOn umfasst sowohl Foundations, als auch Neutralizer, Lidschatten und Rouge: Die mikronisierten Foundations sind in 13 Farbtönen auf Wasser- und 12 auf Silikonbasis erhältlich, zuverlässig deckend und sofort wischfest. Unliebsame Hautverfärbungen (Couperose, Feuermale, Krampfadern o.ä.) lassen sich mit dem Neutralizer in fünf verschiedenen Farbtönen neutralisieren. Für Lidschatten und Rouge bietet SprayOn hochpigmentierte, mikronisierte Farbpigmente an. Die 24 Farben sind wischfest, wasserabweisend und können zur Betonung/Korrektur des Gesichtes, der Augenbrauen und Lippen eingesetzt werden. Sie lassen sich auch mit den Foundations mischen.

SprayOn Airbrush Make-up HD - Aqua Based/Silicone Based

The Airbrush Make-up assortment from SprayOn comprises a foundation as well as a neutralizer, eye shadows and rouge: the micronized foundations are available in 13 water-based and 12 silicon-based colour tones. The wafer-thin application is reliably opaque and immediately smear-resistant. To neutralize possible disagreeable staining on the skin (facial erythrosis, port-wine stains, varicosity) SprayOn offers a neutralizer in 5 different colour tones. As for eye shadows and rouge, SprayOn offers highly pigmented, micronizing colour pigments with an optimal colour choice. The 24 colour tones are smear-resistant and water-repellent, and can be used to underscore the outlines of the face, eyebrows and lips. They can also be mixed with foundations.

Temptu S/B Airbrush Make-up

Temptu S/B Airbrush Make-up ist eine Foundation auf Silikon-Basis, die mittels einer Airbrush-Pistole hauchdünn auf Gesicht, Hals oder Dekolleté aufgetragen wird. Die S/B-Linie lässt sich mit einer 0,35 mm-Düse verarbeiten. 6-8 Tropfen S/B Airbrush Make-up reichen für ein komplettes Make-up aus. Zur Vorbereitung bietet Temptu darüber hinaus einen Moisturizer an, um die Haut mit Feuchtigkeit zu versorgen. Die S/B-Linie verfügt über zwölf Hauttöne (Foundations), vier Rouge-Töne, acht Highlighter, sieben Augenbrauen-Farben sowie insgesamt 13 Bunt- und Korrekturfarben.

Temptu S/B Airbrush Make-up

Temptu S/B Airbrush Make-Up is a silicone-based foundation which can be thinly applied on the face, neck and decollete with an airbrush pistol. The S/B line can be processed with a 0,35 mm nozzle. For the complete make-up, 6-8 drops of the S/B Make-Up are sufficient. Temptu also offers a preparatory moisturizer to supply the skin with enough moisture. The S/B line comprises 12 skin tones (foundations), 4 rouge tones, 8 highlighters, 7 eyebrow colours as well as altogether 13 varicoloured and adjustment colours.

TANNING-LOTIONEN

AviTaN

Der Hersteller von AviTaN legt bei seinem Produkt größten Wert auf Hautpflege. Die Tanning-Lotion kommt ohne Alkohol oder Duftstoff aus und ist daher auch für empfindliche Haut geeignet. AviTaN-Lotionen sind je nach Hauttyp mit einem DHA-Anteil von 8, 10 oder 12 Prozent erhältlich.

TANNING LOTIONS

AviTaN

The manufacturer AviTaN sets high value on skin care. The tanning lotion comes without alcohol and fragrances, and is therefore suitable even for sensitive skin. AviTaN lotions are available with respect to the skin type with a DHA share of 8, 10 or 12 percent.

Mist-Air Premium Tanning

Für ein natürliches, lang anhaltendes Ergebnis besteht die Mist-Air Premium Tanning Lotion aus den Selbstbräunungswirkstoffen DHA und Erythrulose, Aloe sowie weiteren feuchtigkeitsspendenden Inhaltsstoffen zum Schutz der Haut. Mikro-Emulsions-Technologie erlaubt ein effektives Versprühen der Lotion ohne übermäßigen Overspray. Die Lotion ist in den drei Varianten Regular Bronze, Dark und Extra Dark erhältlich. Laut Hersteller tritt der Tanning-Effekt schon nach kürzester Zeit ein, so dass es im Gegensatz zu anderen Tanning-Anwendungen schon nach zwei Stunden möglich ist, wieder eine Dusche zu nehmen. Zum Mist-Air Tanning-Programm gehören darüber hinaus auch spezielle Hautpflege-Produkte wie Duschgels und Feuchtigkeitscremes, die die Haltbarkeit des Tannings unterstützen. Außerdem ist ein Tan-Remover zum Entfernen unerwünschter Tanning-Effekte erhältlich.

Mist-Air Premium Tanning

To reach a natural, long lasting effect, the Mist-Air Premium Tanning Lotion contains the self tanning agents DHA and erythrulose, and aloe as well as other moisturizing ingredients for the skin protection. Microemulsion technology allows for an effective spraying of the lotion without excessive overspray. The lotion is available in the three variants Regular Bronze, Dark and Extra Dark. According to the manufacturer, the tanning effect is visible already after a very short time so that it is possible – opposite to the other tanning applications – to have a shower already after 2 hours. In the Mist-Air Tanning assortment, there are also special skin care products such as shower gels and moisturizing cremes that support the tenability of the tanning. Also a tan remover is available for removing unwanted tanning effects.

FARBEN

Paasche Leisure Tan

Die Paasche Leisure Tan Tanning-Lotion ist geruchs- und parfümfrei und erzielt laut Hersteller eine natürliche Bräunung, die durchschnittlich 5-7 Tage hält. Das Produkt ist je nach Hauttyp und gewünschter Bräunungstiefe mit 8, 10 oder 12 Prozent des Selbstbräunungswirkstoffes DHA erhältlich.

Paasche Leisure Tan

The Paasche Leisure Tan lotion is odourless and perfume-free, and according to the manufacturer helps to attain a natural tanning for an average of 5 to 7 days. According to the skin type and the desired tan´s depth, the product can be obtained with 8, 10 or 12 percent of the self tanning agents DHA.

SprayOn Tanning Lotion

Die Tanning-Lotion wird mit der Airbrush als mikrofeine Zerstäubung gleichmäßig in einem Abstand von ca. 15 cm auf den Körper aufgetragen. Eine Kabine oder eine Haarhaube ist nicht erforderlich, da die Lotion gezielt auf die Haut aufgetragen wird und deshalb kaum Sprühnebel entsteht. Der Verbrauch der Bräunungslösung für eine Behandlung liegt bei ca. 60 ml. Das Tanning hält 5-10 Tage auf der Haut. Die Lotion ist auf Wasserbasis und ohne Öl, Alkohol und Aromastoffe. Sie trocknet sehr schnell. Die Bräunungslösung ist in den drei Farbabstufungen hell, medium und dunkel erhältlich.

SprayOn Tanning Lotion

The tanning lotion is to be applied with an airbrush onto the body as a micro-fine spray from a distance of ca 15 cm. No booth or hair-cover is necessary because the lotion is applied directly onto the skin so that there is only a minimal spraying mist. The consumption of the lotion for one treatment is approximately 60 ml. The tanning lasts on the skin for 5 to 10 days. The lotion is water-based without oil, alcohol and flavors. It dries very quickly. The tanning lotion is available in the three colour grades light, medium and dark.

Yucantan Lotion

Die Tanning-Lotion von Yucantan ist nicht nur schnelltrocknend, sondern überzeugt auch durch die lange Haltbarkeit ihrer Bräunungstönung. Die Lotion ist gut verteilbar und für alle Hauttypen geeignet. Sie beinhaltet keine Öle und Aromastoffe sowie keinen Alkohol. Yucantan Lotion ist in den Bräunungsstufen light, medium und dark erhältlich.

Yucantan Lotion

The Tanning Lotion from Yucantan is not only fast-drying but it also convinces through its long-lasting sustainability of the tanning tone. The lotion is well dispensable and suitable for all skin types. It contains neither oils and flavors nor alcohol. Yucantan Lotion is available in the tanning grades light, medium and dark.

GRUNDÜBUNGEN
BEGINNING EXERCISES

feine Punkte

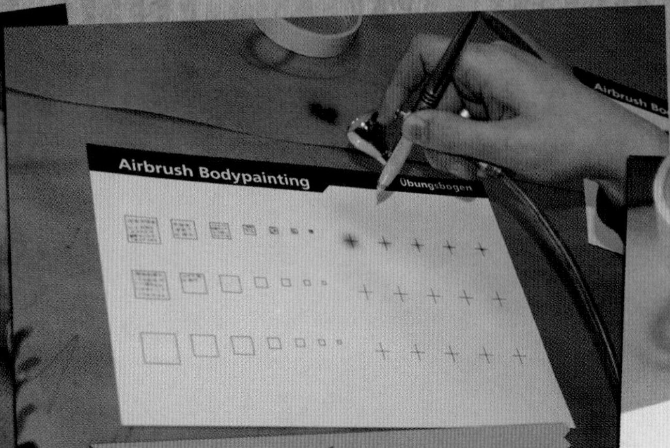

Zielübungen

Verlauf Sprühen

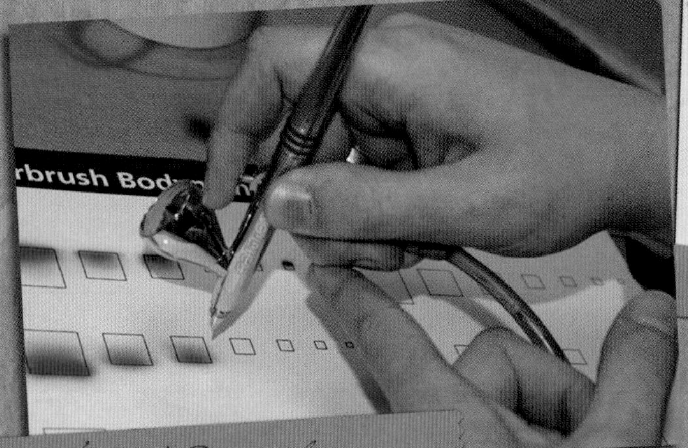

Verlauf Sprühen

IN DEN VERGANGENEN KAPITELN konnten Sie erfahren, welche Ausstattung Sie benötigen. Damit sollten Ihre ersten Vorbereitungen abgeschlossen sein. Um den sicheren Umgang mit dem Airbrushgerät zu erlernen, ist es am besten, sich einfache Techniken anzueignen und zu üben.

In den folgenden Übungen lernen Sie, wie Sie mit dem Gerät umgehen, um immer die ideale Farbmenge zu versprühen. Benutzen Sie für die Übungen einige Bögen weißes Papier und eine normale handelsübliche Airbrush-Acryl-Farbe, bevor es später dann auf die Haut geht.

IN THE PAST CHAPTERS, you could learn about the necessary airbrush equipment. Having passed those lessons, the preparatory theoretical part shall be complete. Now for you to become well-versed in working with an airbrush device, it is the best to adopt some simple techniques and practice.

In the following exercises, you will learn to handle the airbrush device to be able to always spray the right amount of paint. Use for these exercises some sheets of white paper and normal, commercially available acrylic airbrush paints before you start painting on the skin later on.

FUNKTIONSWEISE UND HANDHABUNG DES GERÄTES

Wenn Sie ein Airbrush-Fließsystem benutzen, befüllen Sie den Farbnapf mit einigen Tropfen Farbe. Machen Sie es nicht randvoll, damit die Farbe nicht über den Becherrand schwappt. Arbeiten Sie mit einem Saugsystem, stecken Sie entweder die Farbflasche direkt unter das Gerät oder füllen Sie die Farbe in das dafür vorgesehene Glas oder Becher ein. Arbeiten Sie dann idealerweise an einer Staffelei, damit die Farbe korrekt angesogen wird.

Als Rechtshänder nehmen Sie das Gerät in die rechte Hand. Der Hebel wird mit dem Zeigefinger bedient. In dieser Anleitung gehen wir davon aus, dass Sie mit einem Double-Action-Gerät arbeiten. Mit einem Druck auf den Hebel schalten Sie dieses Gerät sozusagen ein. Nun strömt lediglich Luft durch das Gerät. Sollte nur durch Drücken des Hebels schon Farbe austreten, überprüfen Sie bitte die Düse und die Nadelposition. Wenn Sie den Hebel loslassen, ist das Gerät wieder ausgeschaltet. Ein Zwischenstadium beim Herunterdrücken des Hebels gibt es nicht.

Drücken Sie also den Hebel komplett herunter und ziehen Sie den Hebel dann vorsichtig nach hinten. Sie sehen, wie die Farbe austritt. Je weiter Sie den Hebel nach hinten ziehen, umso mehr Farbe tritt aus.

FUNCTIONING AND HANDLING OF THE DEVICE

If you use the gravity-feed airbrush system, pour a few drops o paint into the colour cup. Do not brim it to avoid colour overflow If you work with the bottom-feed airbrush system, plug the pain bottle in either directly or pour the paint into the colour glass o cup delivered with the airbrush device. Then, work ideally on ar easel so that the paint can be drawn in correctly.

As a right-handed person, take the device into your righ hand and control the trigger with your forefinger. In these instruc tions, we suppose that you are working with a double-action de vice. Putting some pressure onto the trigger, you sort of switch th device on. Now merely the air flows through the device. Shoulc paint come out when the trigger is only pressed, please check the nozzle and the position of the needle. When you release the trig ger, the device is switched off again. There is no half-way stage ir pressing the trigger.

Press the trigger all the way down and than pull it bacl carefully. You can see the paint coming out now. The more yo. pull back the trigger, the more paint comes out.

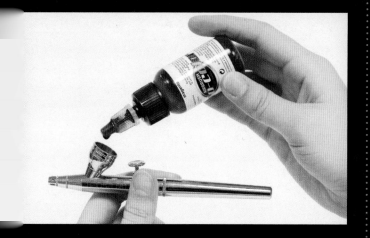

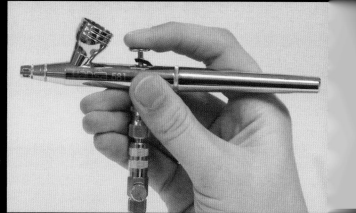

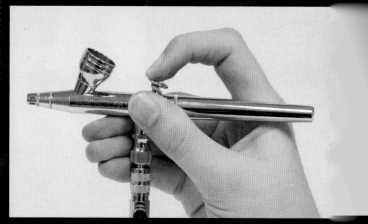

SPRÜHÜBUNGEN

SPRAYING EXERCISES

In der ersten Grundübung geht es um die Bedienung des Airbrushgerätes. Mit Hilfe von Linien können Sie nicht nur den Umgang mit dem Gerät trainieren, sondern auch überprüfen, ob das Airbrushgerät funktionstüchtig ist. Je nach Abstand zum Malgrund können Sie feine Linien oder einen breiten Sprühstrahl mit dem Airbrushgerät erzeugen.

The first basic exercise aims solely at the handling of the airbrush device. With the help of lines, you can exercise yourself not only in handling the device but also you can check if the airbrush device is fully functional. Depending on the distance from the painting ground, you can create very subtle lines or a wide spray pass with the same airbrush device.

Dünne Linien

Dünne Linien erzeugen Sie mit geringem Abstand zum Malgrund. Außerdem halten Sie das Gerät ganz steil, drücken den Hebel herunter und ziehen ihn ganz leicht und vorsichtig nach hinten. Damit Sie keine „Punkte" am Anfang Ihrer Linie erhalten, ist es notwendig, dass Sie den Hebel herunterdrücken und erst in der Bewegung den Hebel nach hinten schieben. So erhalten Sie einen tolles Ein- und Ausfaden der Linie.

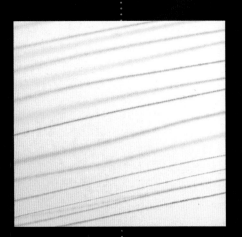

Thin Lines

You create thin lines when the distance between the device and the painting ground is small. Also, you must hold the device very steeply, press the trigger down and pull it back slightly. Be very careful. To avoid spraying globs of paint at the beginning of the line, it is necessary that you press the trigger and only while pressing it, you pull it back. This way you will achieve a great start and finish of the line.

Breite Linien

Breite Linien erreichen Sie mit einem höheren Abstand zum Malgrund. Damit der Farbauftrag stärker zur Geltung kommt, können Sie zusätzlich den Farbhebel weiter nach hinten ziehen. Dadurch wird die Düse weiter geöffnet und mehr Farbe strömt aus. Die Linien müssen nicht glatt und eben sein – das Wichtigste ist, dass man von links beginnt und dann das Gerät nach rechts herüber bewegt. Dann wird die Farbzufuhr gestoppt und man fängt von rechts wieder nach links zu sprühen an. Wenn Sie zwischen den beiden Seiten die Farbzufuhr nicht unterbrechen, erhalten Sie unschöne Farbansammlungen in den Kurven. Dies würde im Motiv später stören.

Wenn Sie beim Farbauftrag mit dem Arm sehr langsam über den Malgrund fahren, kann die Linie ein wenig wellig oder klecksig werden. Bewegen Sie deshalb das Airbrushgerät recht zügig mit dem ganzen Arm über den Malgrund. Diese Linienübung bildet schon mal die Grundlage für spätere Farbverläufe.

Wide Lines

You obtain wide lines when you are working from a bigger distance to your working surface. To underscore the paint application, you can pull the trigger even more to the back. This opens the nozzle wider and more paint will come out. The lines don´t need to be totally smooth and even – the most important thing is that you start on the left side and then move the device to the right side. Then, you stop the paint feed and again start spraying, this time from the right to the left side. When you don´t halt the paint feed between the sides, the paint will accumulate in the curves. This might later mar your motif.

When you – while applying the paint – move your hand above the painting ground very slowly, the line might look somewhat rippled or blotchy. Thus, you need to move the airbrush device more speedy, with the whole arm above the painting ground. This line exercise helps to train your fundamental skills which are later necessary for the work on colour gradients.

Schleifen

Mit der Schleifen-Übung trainieren Sie die Koordination des Airbrushgerätes und können testen, welche Bewegungen und Handgriffe zu welchem Ergebnis führen. Beginnen Sie mit einer geringen Farbmenge mit geringem Abstand zum Malgrund und zeichnen Sie eine Schleife – Sie bekommen eine dünne Schleife. Vergrößern Sie gleichmäßig den Abstand zum Malgrund und ziehen Sie den Hebel ein wenig mehr nach hinten, dann erhalten Sie dickere Schleifen. Sprühen Sie zur Übung einige Schleifen von „dünn nach dick" und direkt wieder von „dick nach dünn". Sie werden sehen: „Übung macht den Meister". Aber auch wenn Sie das Gerät beherrschen, ist es später immer mal wieder notwendig, mit Hilfe der Linien- und Schleifenübung festzustellen, ob das Gerät noch richtig funktioniert oder einzelne Bauteile evtl. verdreckt oder defekt sind.

Loops

Exercising loops will train your skills in coordination of the airbrush device and you will find out the results of certain movements and grips. Start with a little amount of pain from a close distance to the working surface, and create a loop line – you will attain a thin loop line. Scaling up the distance to the painting ground and pulling the trigger back a bit more at the same time, you can create thicker loop lines. To exercise, spray some loops "from thin to thick" and directly "from thick to thin" again. You will see for yourself: "Practice makes perfect". But even if you have mastered the device already, it might be sometimes necessary to test if the device still is fully functional or if eventually some components have got dirty or defect – both of this with the help of line and looping exercises.

Sprühpunkte

Mit dem hier gezeigten Übungsbogen lernen Sie, gezielt Sprühpunkte zu setzen. Ziel der Sprühpunkte-Übung ist es, möglichst viele kleine Sprühsterne auf kleinstem Raum unterzubringen. Dies erreichen Sie, wenn Sie das Gerät senkrecht halten, den Hebel zunächst nur herunterdrücken und dann ganz leicht nach hinten ziehen, so dass nur ein wenig Farbe austritt. Benutzen Sie zur Stabilisierung die linke Hand. Halten Sie das Gerät steil über einen der Punkte mit ca. 5 cm Abstand. Bedenken Sie auch hierbei: Je dichter Sie am Malgrund sind, umso feiner können Sie arbeiten.

Spray Dots

The exercise sheet shown here will help you to create well-directed spray dots. This exercise aims at creating as many spray dots as possible in a very small area. You achieve this when you hold the device in an upright position, press the trigger down and only then slightly pull it back so that some paint comes out. For stabilization, use your left hand. Hold the device in the upright position and ca 5 cm above one of the spots. Remember: The closer to the painting ground you are, the more precision is possible.

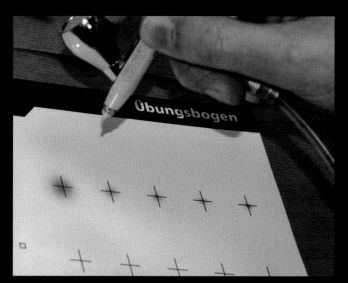

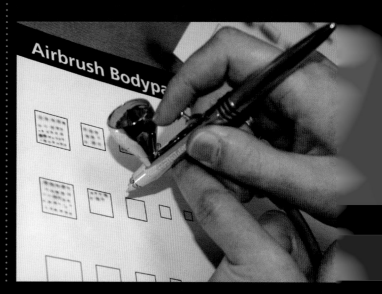

Farbverläufe

Farbverläufe sind besonders schwierig, daher diese wohl wichtigste Koordinationsübung zum Schluss: Grundsätzlich gilt es immer, am Rand des Objektes anzufangen, da es sonst gerade als Anfänger sehr schwierig ist, einen harmonischen Verlauf zu erzeugen. Spritzen Sie die Farbe mit großem Abstand zum Untergrund in gleichmäßigen Bewegungen von links nach rechts sowie von rechts nach links auf. Am Anfang eines Farbverlaufes ist die Farbe stark gesättigt – am Ende sollte der Farbauftrag langsam abnehmen. Durch die Variation des Abstandes gelangt mehr und weniger Farbe auf den Malgrund.

Colour Gradients

Colour gradients are exceptionally difficult, thus you put up with this possibly most important coordination exercise in the end. Basically, the rule is that you should start at the edge of an object because it might otherwise be difficult to create a harmonious gradient. This rule applies especially to beginners. Spray the paint onto the painting ground from a larger distance while steadily moving the device from the left to the right as well as from the right to the left. At the beginning of the colour gradient, the colour is more saturated – at the end, the colour application should slowly decrease. Through the varying distance, you can apply more or less paint onto the working surface.

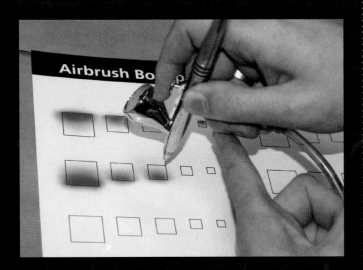

FREIHANDTECHNIK

Speziell beim Bodypainting wird viel mit der Freihand-Airbrush-Technik gearbeitet, bei der Motive quasi „ohne Hilfsmittel gemalt" werden. Diese Arbeitsweise geht schnell und erzeugt je nach Wunsch und Motiv weiche Übergänge, Farbverläufe oder Strukturen. Sie setzt allerdings voraus, dass Sie das Airbrushgerät und die verschiedenen Sprühformen gut beherrschen.

FREE-HAND TECHNIQUE

Especially in body painting you will work a lot with the free-hand technique which means that you will paint the motifs "without auxiliary means". This method, depending on the motif, is quick and able to create soft transitions, colour gradients or structures as desired. However, the precondition is that you have mastered the airbrush device and the various spray forms very well.

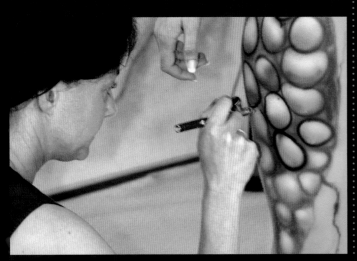

GRUNDÜBUNGEN

LOSE SCHABLONENTECHNIK

Neben der Freihand-Airbrush-Technik wird beim Bodypainting am häufigsten die lose Schablonentechnik eingesetzt. Mit Hilfe von losen Schablonen kann man sehr schnell und variabel scharfkantige Strukturen, Objekte, Motive und Formen erzeugen.

In den Bereichen Airbrush-Tattoos, Hair Art und Nail Art werden vor allem schon vorgefertigte Schablonen benutzt; der Handel bietet dafür unzählige Motive an. Die meisten in Europa erhältlichen losen Schablonen sind aus Mylar. Das ist ein transparentes kunststoffähnliches Folienmaterial, welches mit einem Laserstrahl exakt geschnitten ist. Dank dieser Technik sind auch kleinste Objekte und Muster realisierbar. Die Mylarfolie lässt sich leicht reinigen, hält sehr lange und ist mehrfach verwendbar. Neben Mylar-Schablonen gibt es aber auch Schablonen aus Gummi oder farbigen Kunststoffen, die z.T. noch flexibler sind und demzufolge ein wenig einfacher in der Handhabung.

LOOSE STENCIL TECHNIQUE

Beside the free-hand technique, the loose stencil technique is the most commonly employed technique. With the help of loose stencils, you can create structures with hard-edged lines, objects, motifs and forms very quickly and variably.

In the fields of airbrush tattoos, hair art and nail art, especially ready-made stencils come to benefit; there are countless motifs available in trade. Most of the stencils available in Europe are made out of Mylar. This is a transparent, plastic-like film material, cut out very exactly with a laser jet. This technique allows for creating even the smallest motifs and patterns. The Mylar film is easy to clean, very durable and even reusable. Besides the Mylar stencils, there are also stencils made out of rubber or colourful plastics which are partially even more flexible and hence somewhat easier to handle.

 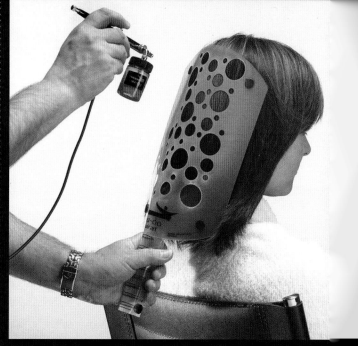

Zum Erzeugen von eigenen losen Schablonen bietet der Airbrushfachhandel Mylarfolie auch als Bogenware an. Mit Hilfe von einem Skalpell oder einem Stencil-Burner (spezielles Gerät, das die Folie durch Hitze schneidet) lassen sich diese Folien bearbeiten. Alternativ lassen sich aber auch Overheadfolien zur Erzeugung einer stabilen transparenten Schablone benutzen. Die günstigste und schnellste Art, Schablonen herzustellen, ist jedoch aus stärkerem Papier oder Pappe. Diese Schablonen werden meist für einmalige Bodypainting-Aktionen, z.B. bei Events oder Wettbewerben verwendet. Indem man das Papier z.B. nicht schneidet, sondern reißt, lassen sich mitunter erstaunliche Effekte erzielen.

Airbrush-specialized trade also offers the Mylar film in sheets to enable you to create your own loose stencils. You can work with this film using a scalpel or a stencil burner (a special device for cutting the film by means of heating up its tip and subsequently melting the film). To create a stable transparent stencil, you can also use overhead foils. However, the cheapest and fastest way to a stencil is a strong paper or cardboard. These stencils are commonly used at one-time body painting activities such as events or competitions. For example, when you don´t cut the paper but tear it, you can achieve some amazing effects.

Lose Schablonentechnik / Loose Stencil Technique

UM DIE ERSTEN ERFAHRUNGEN bei der Motiv-Gestaltung mit Airbrush zu sammeln, ist eine kleine Übungsarbeit auf Papier der beste Einstieg. Hierbei wenden Sie die verschiedenen Sprühmuster praktisch an und üben die Erstellung und Anwendung von Schablonen.

TO COLLECT SOME INITIAL EXPERIENCES in motif design with an airbrush device, it is the best to start with some small exercises on a sheet of paper so that you apply in practice all the different spraying patterns and exercise cutting as well as using the stencils.

VERWENDETE MATERIALIEN

- ▶ 1 Bogen Airbrushpapier
- ▶ Airbrush-Acryl-Farben: Blau, deckendes Weiß, Schwarz
- ▶ Double-Action-Airbrushgerät
- ▶ Einige Bögen Papier für Schablonen
- ▶ Kreisschneider, Cutter
- ▶ Gewichte zur Fixierung

MATERIALS

- ▶ 1 sheet of airbrush paper
- ▶ Airbrush acrylic paints: blue, opaque white, black
- ▶ Double-action airbrush device
- ▶ Several sheets of paper for stencils
- ▶ Circle cutter, cutter
- ▶ Weights for fixation

GRUNDÜBUNGEN

STEP 01

Starten Sie mit einem kleinen bogenförmigen Farbverlauf. Füllen Sie dafür etwas blaue Farbe in den Farbnapf. Im oberen Bereich sprühen Sie etwas dichter (ca. 10 cm) am Malgrund, damit die Farbe gut deckend auf dem Papierbogen aufkommt. Zum Horizont sprühen Sie mit einem größeren Abstand zum Malgrund (ca. 15-20 cm) und mit etwas weniger Farbe (also den Hebel nicht ganz so weit nach hinten ziehen), damit die Farbmenge nach unten hin abnimmt und ein Verlauf entsteht. Sprühen Sie jeweils in Bögen von rechts nach links und von links nach rechts, damit es nicht zu Fleckenbildung kommt.

Begin with a small arch-like colour gradient. For this, load your airbrush with some blue. In the upper area you will spray a bit closer to the painting ground (ca 10 cm) to bring the colour up to enough opaqueness on the sheet of paper. Close to the horizon, spray from a bigger distance to the painting ground (ca 15-20 cm) and with less paint (meaning that you will not pull the trigger back all that much) so that the amount of paint decreases from the bottom up and a colour gradient can develop. Spray with arch-like movements from the right to the left and from the left to the right so to avoid staining.

STEP 02

Jetzt kommt die erste lose Schablone zum Einsatz. Mit einem Bogen Papier wird der gerade gesprühte obere Bereich abgedeckt. Sie können den Bogen mit den Fingern andrücken und festhalten oder auch zu Gewichten greifen, damit die Schablone nicht verrückt. Sprühen Sie die Kante mit Blau ein wenig an. Einige Linien schräg zur Papierkante simulieren die Wasseroberfläche.

At this point, it is time to use the first paper stencil. Cover the upper area with a sheet of paper. You can use fingers to press it against the painting ground and hold it there, or you can also reach out for weights to prevent the stencil from moving. Spray the edge with some blue. Some lines diagonal to the edge of the paper simulate the water surface area.

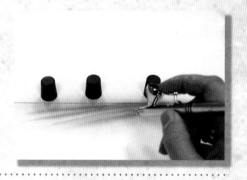

STEP 03

Die lose Papierschablone wird wieder entfernt und der Horizont wird sichtbar. Sie sehen, wie schnell und einfach mit der losen Schablonentechnik Effekte entstehen.

Remove the loose stencil so that the horizon becomes visible. You can see how quickly and simply the effects arise while using the loose stencil technique.

STEP 04

Reißen Sie jetzt aus einem weiteren Bogen Papier eine Bergszenerie heraus. Das geht schnell und erzeugt eine interessante und recht realistische Kante.

Now tear a mountainous scenery out of another sheet of paper. It works quickly and produces interesting and quite realistic edges.

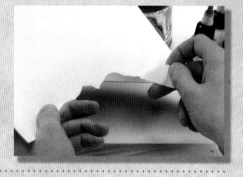

STEP 05

Die äußere Bergschablone wird am Horizont platziert und der untere Bereich mit einem Blatt Papier abgedeckt. Befüllen Sie das Airbrushgerät mit Schwarz und sprühen Sie die entstandene Bergschablone damit aus. Gehen Sie auch hier vorsichtig vor und sprühen Sie in gleichmäßigen Rechts-links- und Links-rechts-Bewegungen. Achten Sie darauf, dass der Farbauftrag nicht zu nass wird und ggf. unter die Schablone läuft.

Place the outward edge of the mountain stencil on the horizon and cover the lower area with a sheet of paper. Load your airbrush device with black and spray it into the created stencil. Proceed very carefully and spray with steady movements rightwards and leftwards. When the colour application is too wet, it gets under the stencil – pay enough attention to avoid this.

STEP 06

Hier sehen Sie den fertigen Zwischenschritt. Wie Sie sicherlich schon bemerkt haben, ist ein weiterer Vorteil der losen Schablonentechnik, dass Sie recht flexibel die Schablone auflegen und so die Höhe der Berggruppe schnell ändern können.

What you can see here is the finished intermediate step. You have certainly noticed that another advantage of the loose stencil technique lies in the possibility to place the stencil very flexibly which enables you to change the height of the mountain quickly.

STEP 07

Reißen Sie eine weitere Bergszenerie aus einem Bogen Papier heraus, um den Vordergrund zu formen. Legen Sie die Schablone unterhalb der Meereswellen an. Sprühen Sie ebenfalls mit Schwarz die Ränder der Schablone an und geben Sie dem Gebilde etwas Volumen. Nach unten hin lassen Sie die Farbe auslaufen.

Tear another mountainous scenery out of a paper sheet to shape the foreground. Place the stencil underneath the sea waves. Also here, spray the edge of the stencil black and give the formation some volume. Let the colour fade out.

STEP 08

Nicht nur durch Reißen können interessante Strukturen und Formen erzeugt werden. Natürlich können Sie auch direkt Motive auf starkem Papier aufzeichnen und mit einem Skalpell ausschneiden. In diesem Fall habe ich eine Palme gezeichnet, die anschließend ausgeschnitten wurde.

Not only the tearing allows you to create interesting structures and shapes. Naturally, you can also directly draw a motif on some strong paper and cut it out with a scalpel. In this case, I drew a palm tree and cut it out.

STEP 09

Jetzt wird die Palmenschablone auf die Berge im Vordergrund platziert und mit Schwarz ausgesprüht. Benutzen Sie die Finger oder Gewichte, um evtl. Teilbereiche der Schablone festzudrücken. Stellen Sie sicher, dass um die Palme herum ausreichend Papier das Motiv abdeckt, um zu vermeiden, dass sich Farbnebelränder über dem Motiv bilden.

You can now place the palm tree stencil onto the mountains in the foreground and spray it black. Use the fingers or the weights to press down the stencil if necessary. Make sure that there is enough paper covering the rest of the motif around the palm tree to protect it from colour overspray.

STEP 10

Hier sehen Sie das Ergebnis. Zusätzlich wurden freihand ein paar Grashalme eingesprüht. Dünne Freihand-Linien sind schwierig, deshalb ist es ratsam, auf einem Stück Papier vorher einige Linien zu üben. Halten Sie das Gerät recht steil am Malgrund und ziehen Sie dünne Linien von unten nach oben in das Bild hinein.

Here you can see the result. In addition, spray some blades of grass free-hand. Thin free-hand lines are very difficult to create, and you might want to practice some lines of this kind on a sheet of paper beforehand. Hold the device quite steeply above the painting ground and create thin lines on the picture in a bottom-up manner.

STEP 11

Mit einem Kreisschneider wird die nächste lose Schablone hergestellt. Legen Sie diese Schablone dann im oberen Bereich des Himmels an. Unten rechts sprühen Sie in den Kreis vorsichtig eine Lichtkante ein. Halten Sie das Gerät dazu steil und in einem Abstand von 8-10 cm vom Malgrund entfernt.

Use a circle cutter to create another loose stencil. Place this stencil in the upper sky area. Carefully spray a light edge into the circle down to the right. Hold the device steeply again and respect that the necessary distance from the painting ground is now ca 8-10 cm.

STEP 12

Um dem Planeten eine Struktur zu verpassen, gibt es unterschiedliche Möglichkeiten. Die einfachste ist, dünne Linien vom Planetenrand aus zittrig einzuziehen. Das Gerät dazu ganz dicht am Malgrund halten, die Farbzufuhr nur ganz wenig und vorsichtig öffnen und unterschiedlich lange, zittrige Linien einsprühen.

To give the planet some structure, you can choose from various possibilities. The simplest one is to create thin, shaky lines starting at the edge of the planet. To accomplish this, hold the device really closely to the working surface, carefully open the paint feed only a tiny bit, and spray some shaky lines of different length.

STEP 13

Für eine sternenklare Sommernacht werden jetzt mit Weiß „Sterne gesprenkelt". Das Sprenkeln mit dem Airbrushgerät erzeugt für viele Motive einen interessanten Effekt. Nicht nur Galaxien, sondern auch Steinstrukturen, die beim Bodypainting häufig Anwendung finden, lassen sich damit erzeugen. Es gibt einige Hilfsmittel wie z.B. Schnellkupplung mit Luftregulierung, Sprenkelkappe oder Wäscheklammer, um mit dem Airbrushgerät zu sprenkeln. Um aber ohne Hilfsmittel mit möglichst wenig Aufwand schnell und gezielt einen Sprenkel-Effekt zu erzielen, empfehlen wir hier die Schlauchabknickmethode.

Dazu knicken Sie den Schlauch ab und drücken den Airbrushhebel von vorne nach hinten schnell durch. Um immer ein wenig Luft zum Sprenkeln in das Gerät zu lassen, öffnen und schließen Sie den Schlauchknick durch Pumpen. Diese Methode erfordert ein wenig Übung, da gleichzeitig der Schlauch jeweils stark/weniger stark geknickt wird und dann noch der Hebel schnell gedrückt und nach hinten gezogen werden muss. Einige Airbrushgeräte lassen es auch zu, dass der Bedienhebel nur nach hinten gezogen wird, ohne diesen herunterzudrücken, um Sprenkler zu bekommen. Eine weitere Methode lernen Sie in den späteren Workshops.

To create an impression of a starlit summer night, you can now "sprinkle the stars" using some white. The sprinkling with an airbrush device has an interesting effect on many motifs. It can give rise to not only galaxies but also stone structures which are very common in body painting. There are some auxiliary means such as a quick coupling with air control, a sprinkler head or a clothes-peg to sprinkle with an airbrush. However, to achieve a sprinkling effect with the least possible effort and without any auxiliary means, we recommend the squeeze method.

This method means that you squeeze the air hose and quickly pull the airbrush trigger back. To let some air into the device to sprinkle, open and close the hose squeeze in a pumping way. This method requires some practice because the hose must be strongly or less strongly squeezed, and the trigger must be quickly pressed and pulled back, all that at once. Some airbrush devices also let you to only pull the trigger back without pressing it, and still create the sprinkles. In the following workshops, you will also learn another method.

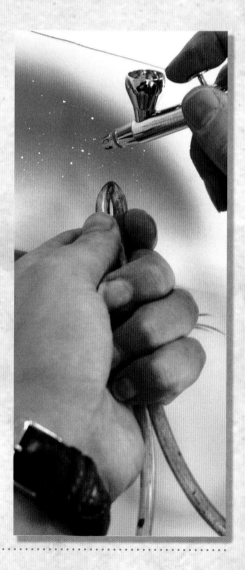

STEP 14

Lassen Sie die Sterne gut trocknen. Verzieren Sie dann einige Punkte mit einem Sprühpunkt, um diese zum Leuchten zu bringen. Benutzen Sie die linke Hand zur Stabilisierung. Im Abstand von ca. 5 cm halten Sie das Gerät steil und drücken zunächst nur den Knopf komplett runter, um Luft zu geben. Dann ziehen Sie den Hebel vorsichtig und ganz wenig nach hinten, um den Sprühpunkt zu erzeugen.

Let the stars dry properly. Garnish some points with a spray dot to light them up. Use the left hand for more stability. Hold the device steeply in a distance of ca 5 cm and press the trigger completely to provide air. Then, pull the trigger carefully and only slightly to the back to create the spray dot.

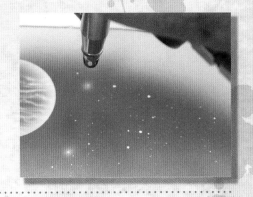

STEP 15

Um einen funkelnden Stern zu simulieren, schneiden Sie mit einem Lineal ein dünnes aber gerades Kreuz aus. Setzen Sie dazu das Lineal an, schneiden Sie 4-5 cm. Versetzen Sie das Lineal dann parallel um 1 bis 2 Millimeter nach links und schneiden Sie dort ebenfalls ein. Drehen Sie jetzt das Lineal um 90 Grad und schneiden Sie dasselbe nochmal. Die letzten Ecken können dann freihändig herausgeschnitten werden.

To simulate a twinkling star, cut out a thin but straight cross with a ruler. To do this, put the ruler into a position and cut 4 to 5 cm. Then, move the ruler 1 to 2 mm to the left and cut the same way. Now rotate the ruler at 90° and cut again. The rest of the corners you can then cut free-hand.

STEP 16

Legen Sie die neue Sternenschablone horizontal an und sprühen Sie mit einem Abstand von 5-8 cm ganz vorsichtig ein wenig Weiß in die Mitte des Kreuzes auf. Auf keinen Fall komplett ausmalen, da sich die Farbe durch den Sprühkegel automatisch in den Balken verstreuen soll. Nehmen Sie anschließend die Schablone ab und sprühen Sie vorsichtig in die Mitte des Kreuzes einen Sprühpunkt, um den Stern zum Leuchten zu bringen.

Place the new star stencil horizontally and spray from a distance of 5 to 8 cm very carefully a little bit of white into the middle of the cross. Do not completely paint it because the paint should be distributed across the arms as you simply spray the jet. Subsequently, remove the stencil and spray carefully a spray dot into the middle of the cross to make the star twinkle brighter.

STEP 17

Im letzten Schritt werden freihand mit Weiß noch einige Schaumkronen auf den Wellen ergänzt. Gehen Sie dabei ähnlich vor wie bei den Planetenstrukturen. Sprühen Sie aus der Bewegung heraus, damit die zittrigen Linien am Ende leicht ausfaden. Ebenfalls mit gezitterten Linien formen Sie die Konturkante der Wolkengebilde und füllen diese anschließen mit Volumen auf. Bei diesem Motiv konnten Sie selbst erleben, wie einfach der Umgang mit losen Schablonen ist und wie schnell sich eigene Motive damit formen lassen.

In the last step, work freehand and use some white to create some foam on the waves. You can work here in a similar way as you did while creating the structures of the planets. Spray out of the movement so that the shaky lines can fade out. Using the same shaky lines, you can also create the edges of the clouds and fill them subsequently with volume. While working on this motif, you could see for yourself how easy the work with loose stencils is and how fast you can shape your own motifs with their help.

FREIHANDTECHNIK
FREEHANDTECHNIQUE

DIE FREIHANDTECHNIK ist die Grundlage jeden Motivs, um Schattierung, Tiefe und Plastizität zu erzeugen. Sie erfordert jedoch eine sichere Kontrolle des Airbrushgerätes und zielgenaues, dosiertes Versprühen der Farbe. Mit einem einfachen Motiv können Sie diese Fähigkeiten weiter verbessern.

THE FREE-HAND TECHNIQUE is the basis of any motif as far as for the shadings, depth and plasticity. However, it requires a confident handling of the airbrush device and a pinpointed, well dosed spraying of the paint. You can enhance your skills with the following simple motif.

VERWENDETE MATERIALIEN

- ▶ 1 Bogen Airbrushpapier
- ▶ Airbrush-Acryl-Farben: Grün, deckendes Weiß, Schwarz
- ▶ Double-Action-Airbrushgerät
- ▶ Kreppband zum Maskieren des Arbeitsbereiches

MATERIALS

- ▶ 1 sheet of airbrush paper
- ▶ Airbrush acrylic paints: green, opaque white, black
- ▶ Double-action airbrush device
- ▶ Adhesive tape for masking of the working space

STEP 01

Grenzen Sie einen Teil Ihres Airbrushkartons durch Maskierung ab. Sie können die Größe selbst bestimmen; je größer der Bereich, umso länger dauert die Übungseinheit. Mischen Sie sich dann ein sehr transparentes Schwarz aus etwa einem Tropfen Schwarz und 10-20 Tropfen Wasser. Sie erhalten einen grauen Farbton. Sprühen Sie mit dieser Farbe ungleichmäßig Stein- bzw. Schuppenformen auf. Die Objekte sollen sich jeweils berühren. Kleine Zwischenräume werden später mit Schwarz ausgefüllt. Versuchen Sie beim Ansetzen der jeweiligen Umrandungen Sprühpunkte zu vermeiden.

Define a certain area on the airbrush cardboard with a mask. You can define the size of this area yourself; the larger the area, the longer the exercise will take you. Then, mix a very transparent black using about one drop of black and about 10-20 drops of water. You will obtain a grey colour tone. With this colour, spray unevenly stone or respectively scaling shapes. The objects should be touching each other. Small interspaces will later be filled with black. Try to avoid spraying dots while spraying the edges.

STEP 02

Mit der gleichen Mischung sprühen Sie innerhalb der einzelnen Kreisformen unten und rechts eine Schattierung ein. Nehmen Sie das Gerät dazu etwas höher. Bestimmen Sie die Intensität der Schattierung durch mehrmaliges Übernebeln. Lassen Sie noch ein wenig Licht in den Bereichen stehen.

With the same mix, spray a shading within the individual circles on the right bottom side. For this, increase the distance between the device and the working surface a little bit. Define the intensity of the shadings through overspraying it again and again. Leave still some light leftovers in the areas.

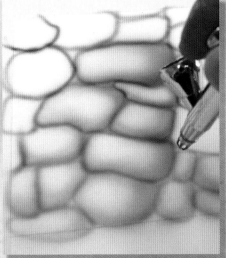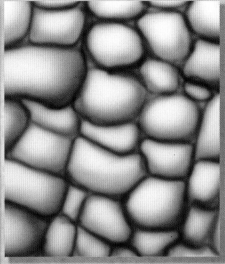

STEP 03

Mit einer transparenten Farbe Ihrer Wahl werden jetzt die Schattenbereiche übergenebelt. Durch das Overspray gelangt der gewählte Farbton auch ein wenig in die helleren Bereiche und gibt dem Motiv insgesamt Farbe.

Now overspray the area of the shadings with a transparent colour of your choice. Through this overspray, some of the chosen colour tone will appear also in the lighter areas and will colour up the whole motif.

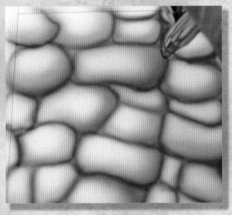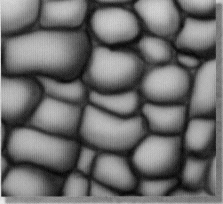

STEP 04

Mit Weiß können zum Schluss noch Lichtpunkte herausgearbeitet werden. Benutzen Sie deckendes Weiß und sprühen Sie es vorsichtig in die hellen Bereiche ein. Ziehen Sie anschließend die Maskierung ab.

Finally, you can also work out some light spots with white. Use opaque white and spray it carefully into the light areas. Subsequently, remove the masking.

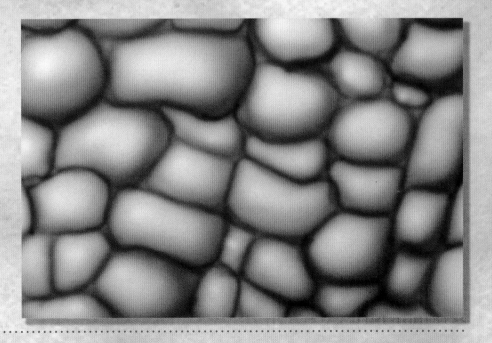

AIRBRUSH TATTOOS

IN DEN ERSTEN KAPITELN konnten Sie sich bereits einen Überblick über die verschiedenen Anwendungsbereiche der Airbrush-Technik am Körper verschaffen. Nachdem jetzt auch die Grundlagen hinsichtlich der Airbrush-Ausstattung und ersten Übungen mit dem Gerät geschaffen sind, kann es mit der Anwendung am Körper losgehen. Bevor Sie sich an komplexe Ganzkörper-Bodypaintings wagen, beginnen Sie zunächst mit Tattoos und Make-up. Die Arbeit auf vergleichsweise kleinen Flächen mit Unterstützung von Schablonen erleichtert den Einstieg.

IN THE ABOVE CHAPTERS, you could get a rough idea of the various application fields of the airbrush techniques in body painting. The basics of the airbrush equipment have been explained and the basic exercises illustrated, so let´s rock and paint the bodies! Before you dare to approach some complex whole body paintings, begin with tattoos and make-up. Working on relatively small areas with the support of stencils is going to be the easier kind of start.

Airbrush-Tattoos halten bei guter Platzierung, Ausführung und Farbe in der Regel rund 2-3 Tage, was sie sowohl unter Erwachsenen als auch Jugendlichen zu einem beliebten Körperschmuck, Party-Gag und Veranstaltungsattraktion machen. Die Haltbarkeit des Tattoos hängt neben der verwendeten Farbe, der Vorbereitung und dem Hauttyp vor allem von der Körperstelle ab, auf die es aufgetragen wird. Ein Airbrush-Tattoo unter einem Hosen- oder Ärmel-Bündchen hat z.B. aufgrund der Reibung keine lange Überlebenschance. Außerdem sollte beim Duschen darauf geachtet werden, dass keine Seife oder Bodylotion an das Motiv gelangt.

Größte Sorgfalt sollte auch bei der Auswahl der Farbe herrschen. Gerade wenn Airbrush-Tattoos auf großen Veranstaltungen bei vielen Menschen – von jung bis alt – angewendet werden, sollte man auf zuverlässig getestete und zertifizierte Farben zurückgreifen (siehe Seite 34/35). Passende Schablonen bieten viele Farbhersteller, aber auch spezialisierte Schablonenhersteller (im Internet leicht zu finden) an. Wer sich nur auf Airbrush-Tattoos spezialisieren möchte, ist ggf. mit einem der vielen angebotenen Tattoo-Komplett-Sets mit Airbrushgerät, Kompressor, Schablonen und Farben gut und günstig bedient. In den USA gibt es sogar ganze „Business-Start-Up"-Angebote, die vom Werbeaufsteller über Verkaufstresen bis hin zu Tisch und Stühlen gleich das ganze Event-Equipment gleich mitliefern.

Provided an appropriate spot and colour and carried out in an appropriate manner, airbrush tattoos last usually about 2-3 days which makes them a popular body decoration, party gag and event attraction for the youngsters as well as for the adults. How long the tattoo will last depends also on the used colour, preparation and the skin type, and above all on the spot where the tattoo is applied. For example, an airbrush tattoo beneath the trousers or sleeve waistband has naturally no great chance of survival. Besides, it is important to remember that while taking a shower, no soap or body lotion should get onto the motif.

Of course, the choice of the paint should be ruled by the greatest diligence. It is exactly because the airbrush tattoos are being applied onto many people – young or old – at the big events why we should always use reliably tested and certified paints (see pages 34/35). The suitable stencils can be obtained from many manufactures of paints but also from the specialized stencil manufacturers (easy to find on the Internet). Who wishes to specialize in airbrush tattoos, he or she might feel well served with one of the many reasonably priced tattoo complete sets which include an airbrush device, compressor, stencils and paints. To be found in the USA, there are even complete "Business-Start-Up" offers which provide all the necessary event equipment ranging from the advertising panels and selling counters up to the tables and chairs.

AUFTRAGEN EINES AIRBRUSH-TATTOOS
APPLICATION OF AIRBRUSH TATTOOS

VERWENDETE MATERIALIEN:

- ▶ Tattoo-Farbe Schwarz
- ▶ Airbrushgerät
- ▶ Tattoo-Schablonen
- ▶ Fixierpuder
- ▶ Pinsel
- ▶ Isopropylalkohol

MATERIALS

- ▶ Black tattoo paint
- ▶ Airbrush device
- ▶ Tattoo stencils
- ▶ Fixing powder
- ▶ Paintbrush
- ▶ Isopropyl alcohol

STEP 01

Zuerst wird die Airbrush-Tattoo-Schablone ausgewählt. Sprechen Sie dann die Körperstelle und Position des geplanten Tattoos mit Ihrem „Modell" ab.

Choose the tattoo stencil and agree with your model on the adequate spot and position of the tattoo.

STEP 02

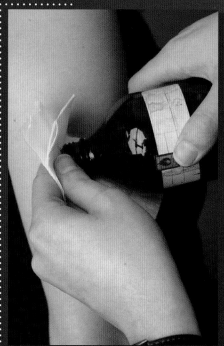

Damit ein Airbrush-Tattoo möglichst lange hält, wird die Haut mit Alkohol gründlich entfettet. Hierbei kann 75- oder 99-prozentiger Isopropylalkohol aus der Apotheke verwendet werden.

To make an airbrush tattoo last as long as possible, the skin should be well degreased with alcohol. You can use a 75% or 99% isopropyl alcohol which is commonly available at the chemist.

TATTOOS

STEP 03

STEP 04

STEP 05

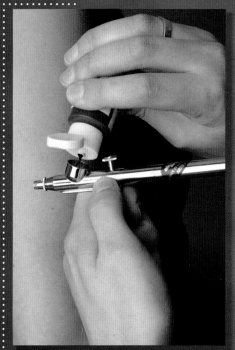

Vor dem Farbauftrag ausreichend Tattoo-Farbe in den Farbbehälter füllen. Nichts ist ärgerlicher, als wenn man zwischendurch nachfüllen muss. Arbeitet man bei einer größeren Veranstaltung und rechnet mit vielen Tattoos innerhalb kürzester Zeit, ist es ratsam, mit einem Airbrush-Saugsystem zu arbeiten. Das garantiert ein reibungsloses Sprühen ohne nachzufüllen.

Mit der linken Hand wird die Schablone fixiert, mit der rechten Hand das Airbrushgerät bedient. Das Motiv wird schrittweise mit der Tattoo-Farbe ausgesprüht. Je nach Schablone und Geschick kann dabei Overspray entstehen. Dieser kann zwar später entfernt werden, dennoch ist es wichtig, das Motiv möglichst scharfkantig auf die Haut aufzutragen. Hat die vorhandene Schablone sehr wenig Rand, können Sie diese mit Klebeband und Tuch/Papier erweitern. Sprühen Sie die Farbe in mehreren Schichten und nicht zu nass auf. Bei großen Motiven müssen Sie ggf. zwischendurch an der Schablone nachfassen, um sie an anderer Stelle besser andrücken zu können.

Nach der Entfernung der Tattoo-Schablone lässt sich das fertige Tattoo begutachtet. Overspray, das über den Schablonenrand hinaus gegangen ist, kann mit einem Tuch oder Pad und Alkohol oder Babyöl entfernt werden.

Load your airbrush with a sufficient amount of paint before you start spraying. There is nothing more annoying than being forced to interrupt the work to top up the paint. When you are working at some big events and expect to create many tattoos within a really short time, it is recommended to work with a bottom-feed airbrush system. It ensures smooth spraying without a need for refill.

Place the stencil into position with your left hand and operate the airbrush device with your right hand. Gradually spray the tattoo motif with the tattoo paint. Depending on your skills and on the stencil, there might be some overspray. Although this overspray can be removed later on, it is important to apply the motif on the skin as hard-edged as possible. When the stencil has only a small verge, you can broaden it with some adhesive tape and tissue/paper. Apply the paint in several layers and not all-too wet. When you are working on a large motif, it might be necessary to follow up the stencil and press it with your hand on appropriate spots.

Having removed the stencil, you can render an opinion to the final result. You can also remove the overspray which crossed the edges of the stencil with a tissue or pad and alcohol or baby oil.

STEP 06

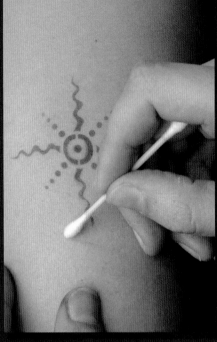

Sollten Details korrigiert werden müssen, hat man mit einem Wattestäbchen die Möglichkeit dazu. Wattestäbchen in Alkohol tauchen und vorsichtig überflüssige Farbe abreiben.

If some detailed adjustments are necessary, use a cotton bud. Dip it into alcohol and carefully rub off the superfluous paint.

STEP 07

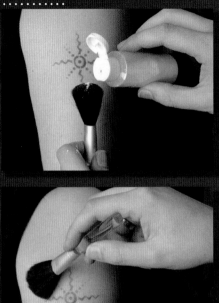

Um die Haltbarkeit zu unterstützen, wird das Motiv mit einem Fixierpuder (oder alternativ Babypuder) abgepudert. Ein wenig Puder wird auf einen weichen Pinsel geträufelt und dann vorsichtig verteilt.

To make the tattoo last longer, powder the motif with a fixing powder (or also baby powder). Using a soft paintbrush, apply some powder carefully onto the tattoo.

STEP 08

Das Motiv ist nun geschützt. Auch Duschen ist jetzt u.U. möglich, danach sollte das Tattoo aber erneut abgepudert werden, um die Haltbarkeit zu verbessern. Das komplette Entfernen des Airbrush-Tattoos ist ganz einfach: Nur mit Alkohol oder Öl abreiben.

The motif is now secured. Even taking a shower is possible. However afterwards, some powder should be applied again to make the tattoo last longer. It is very easy to completely remove the tattoo: simply rub it off with alcohol or oil.

TATTOOS

TATTOO: ORIGINAL UND FÄLSCHUNG

NACH DEM VORANGEGANGENEN STEP BY STEP wissen Sie, wie man Airbrush-Tattoos auf die Haut aufbringt. Jetzt möchten wir Ihnen eine reizvolle Ergänzung zum bloßen Aussprühen von Tattoo-Schablonen zeigen: Wie wär's damit, ein echtes Tattoo einfach fortzusetzen? Mit Tattoo-Folie und -Farbe können Sie dies ganz einfach realisieren. Wer weiß dann noch, welches echt oder nur aufgesprüht ist?

TATTOO: ORIGINAL AND FAKE

HAVING READ THE ABOVE STEP-BY-STEP, you know how to apply an airbrush tattoo on the skin. At this point, we would like to show an appealing extension of mere spraying of tattoo stencils: How about upgrading real tattoos? You can do this simply by using a tattoo foil and tattoo paint. Who can then tell what's real and what's the fake?

VERWENDETE MATERIALIEN

- ▶ Schwarze Tattoo-Farbe
- ▶ Airbrushgerät
- ▶ Vorbereitete Tattoo-Folie
- ▶ Fixierpuder
- ▶ Pinsel

MATERIALS

- ▶ *Black tattoo paint*
- ▶ *Fixing powder*
- ▶ *Paintbrush*
- ▶ *Airbrush device*
- ▶ *Prepared tattoo foil*

Hier sehen Sie die fertige Komposition der beiden Tattoo-Motive.

Here you can see the finished composition of the two tattoo motifs.

STEP 01

Damit das zu ergänzende Tattoo-Motiv scharfkantig auf den Körper aufgetragen werden kann, verwenden Sie eine klebende Folie. Als Materialien kommt handelsübliche Plotter-Klebefolie mit zugehöriger Transferfolie zum Einsatz. Beachten Sie dabei, dass evtl. Klebstoffallergien beim Modell auftreten können.

Use an adhesive film to be able to apply the additional tattoo motif onto the skin with hard-edges. You can use the plotter adhesive foil and the appropriate transfer foil, both available in trade. Remember that potential allergic reactions could occur while using the foil on the skin of the model.

STEP 02

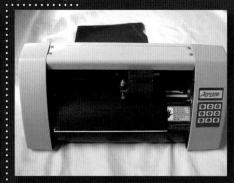

Hier sehen Sie einen einfachen Schneidplotter. Diese Geräteart zur Herstellung von Schablonen und Beschriftungen gibt es in unterschiedlichen Ausführungen, Größen und Preisklassen. Alternativ können Sie sich Ihr Tattoo-Motiv auch bei jeder Werbefirma vor Ort ausplotten lassen. Das ist auf alle Fälle günstiger, vor allem wenn Sie nur ab und zu eine klebende Schablone benötigen.

Here you can see a simple cutter plotter. There are various kinds of this device for creating stencils and labels in different size and price ranges. You can also ask any local advertising company to plot your tattoo motif for you. It is on all accounts cheaper especially if you only need an adhesive stencil occasionally.

STEP 03

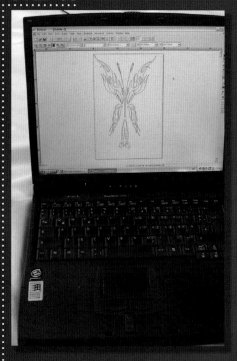

Neben der schon aufgeführten Hardware benötigen Sie zusätzlich entsprechende Software, um Ihr Motiv zu gestalten und auf den Plotter auszugeben. Hierbei werden sogenannte Vektorgrafikprogramme benutzt wie z.B. Adobe Illustrator, Freehand oder CorelDraw.

In addition to the above listed hardware, you also need the appropriate software to design your motif and pass it on to the plotter. For this purpose, it is common to use the so called vector graphics software such as the Adobe Illustrator, Freehand or CorelDraw.

TATTOOS

STEP 04

Planen Sie vorher die korrekte Größe, damit das ergänzende Tattoo-Motiv zu dem vorhandenen passt. Bei der Verwendung einer Vektorgrafik können Sie das Motiv jederzeit ohne Qualitätsverlust auf das gewünschte Format vergrößern. Wenn Sie die Möglichkeit haben, mit einer Bildbearbeitungssoftware zu arbeiten, können Sie das geplante Motiv auch schon vorher digital auf das Personenfoto montieren, um einen ersten Eindruck des Gesamtmotivs zu erhalten.

Plan the right size beforehand so that the tattoo extension motif fits the real tattoo. Using the vector graphics, it is possible to bring the motif into the desired size any time and at no quality loss. When you have the possibility to work with an image editing software, you can also digitally assemble the intended motif on the photo of the particular person to gain some initial impression of the motif as a whole.

STEP 05

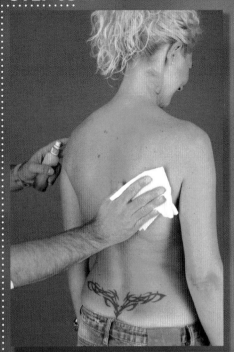

Damit das Tattoo-Motiv eine Weile auf dem Körper hält, wird die Haut vorher mit Alkohol entfettet.

The skin must be degreased with alcohol so that the tattoo lasts on the body for some time.

STEP 06

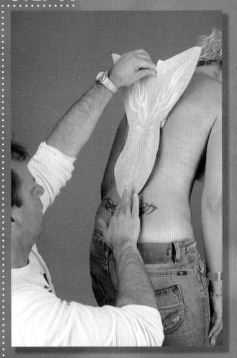

Positionieren Sie jetzt die Tattoo-Schablone, ziehen Sie einen Teil der Transferfolie im unteren Bereich ab und kleben Sie sie auf.

Position the tattoo stencil, pull off some transfer foil at the bottom and affix it.

STEP 07

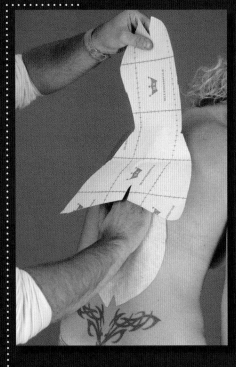

Ist der untere Teil fixiert, kann nun der obere Bereich abgezogen werden.

Having affixed the bottom part of the stencil, you can pull off the rest of the transfer foil.

STEP 08

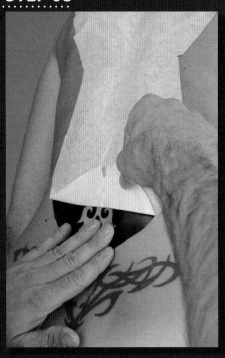

Ziehen Sie jetzt vorsichtig die Transferfolie ab. Da diese klebende Folie auf dem Körper keine so starke Haftung hat, ist es ratsam, mit der Hand die klebende Folie jeweils ein wenig zu fixieren, während Sie die Transferfolie abziehen. Überprüfen Sie dann nochmal den Halt und die einzelnen Bestandteile der Maskierung, bevor Sie mit dem Airbrushgerät starten.

Carefully pull off the transfer foil. Because the adhesive film cannot be firmly attached to the body, you are well advised if you fixate it with your hand while pulling off the transfer foil. And then, check again the hold of the stencil and all the parts of the masking before you trigger off your airbrush device.

STEP 09

Füllen Sie die gewünschte Tattoo-Farbe in Ihr Airbrushgerät ein. Je nach Größe des Motivs benötigen Sie mehrere Tropfen Farbe.

Load your airbrush device with the desired colour. Depending on the size of the motif, you will need several drops of the paint.

TATTOOS

STEP 10

Sprühen Sie nun vorsichtig die Schablone aus. Achten Sie dabei darauf, dass Sie nicht über den Maskierfolienrand sprühen. Bauen Sie das Motiv ruhig in mehreren Schichten auf und sprühen Sie die Farbe nicht zu nass auf.

Carefully spray the paint into the stencil openings. Pay attention and try not to spray over the verge of the masking film. You can smoothly develop the motif layer by layer but always remember not to spray all-too wet.

STEP 11

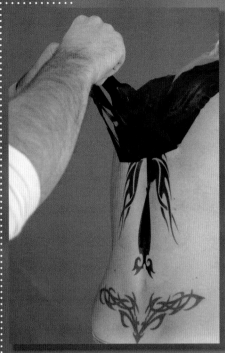

Wenn die Farbe trocken ist, können Sie die Schablone behutsam abziehen.

Let the colour dry and gently pull off the stencil.

STEP 12

Sollte Overspray entstanden sein, können Sie diesen mit einem Tuch und Isopropylalkohol oder Körperöl entfernen. Zur Fixierung benutzen Sie Fixierpuder und einen Pinsel.

If there is some overspray, you can now remove it with a cloth and isopropyl alcohol or body oil.
Use fixing powder and a paintbrush for fixation.

Airbrush Make-up

Neue Technologien stellen Maskenbildner und Make-up Artists, die vorrangig für Film und Fernsehen arbeiten, immer wieder vor neue Herausforderungen. Die Entwicklung der hochauflösenden HDTV-Technik ist wahrscheinlich nach der Einführung des Farbfilms eine der bahnbrechendsten Erfindungen. Während das Standard-Fernsehprogramm Bilder mit einer Auflösung von etwa 788 x 576 Bildpunkten (576 Zeilen im Zeilensprungmodus) bereitstellt, liefert das Volldigital-Bild eine Auflösung von 1920 x 1080 Bildpunkten (1080 Zeilen in Zeilensprungmodus). Mehr und damit kleinere Bildpunkte liefern also ein schärferes und kontrastreicheres Bild als bisher und machen daher viele Details, Strukturen und Konturen sichtbar, die bisher den groberen Bildpunkten zum Opfer fielen. Dementsprechend müssen auch Make-up-Farben – sowohl im Special Effects Bereich als auch die normale Foundation – noch feiner als die bisher grobpigmentierten Puder wirken.

Mask-building artists as well as make-up artists who mainly work in the movie and TV field are constantly challenged by new technologies. The development of the high definition HDTV-technique has probably been one of the major breakthroughs following the technicolor movies. While the standard TV picture resolution is about 788 x 576 pixels (576 rows in the interlace mode), the fully digital picture can be presented with a resolution of 1920 x 1080 pixels (1080 rows in the interlace mode). More and smaller pixels give a sharper and highly contrasted picture. And hence, even those rich details, structures and contours become visible which fell pray to the lower resolution in the past. Correspondingly, the make-up must be finer than the previously not as fine ground powder pigments – in the field of special effects as well as with a normal foundation.

Die Zerstäubung von feinpigmentierten Flüssigfarben mit der Airbrush-Technik bietet hier die rettende Lösung. Allerdings zeigt sich die Airbrush-Technik hinsichtlich ihrer voluminösen und schweren Ausstattung im Visagistenalltag weniger flexibel als sonstiges Schminkequipment und verlangt von den Make-up Artists, eine völlig neue Anwendung zu erlernen.

Airbrush-Make-up-Farben für Foundations, Lidschatten, Rouge und Fantasy-Make-ups werden üblicherweise gebrauchsfertig für das Airbrushgerät ausgeliefert. Foundations lassen sich deckend oder transparent auftragen. Trotz der dünnen Farbschicht lassen sie durch die hohe Pigmentierung Fältchen, Pickel, Narben und Altersflecken einfach und nachhaltig verschwinden.

Um Airbrush-Make-up aufzutragen, empfiehlt sich eine Airbrushpistole ab einer Düsengröße von 0,2 mm bis maximal 0,5 mm. Da meist ein einziger Tropfen Farbe ausreicht, um das Gesicht abzudecken, stellt ein Fließsystem mit kleinem Farbnapf genügend Farbe zur Verfügung. Die Einstellung des Arbeitsdrucks am Kompressor sollte 0,7 bar nicht übersteigen, damit die Make-up-Pigmente fast trocken auf die Haut gelangen. Darüber hinaus wird der Luftstrahl im Gesicht stärker wahrgenommen als an anderen Stellen des Körpers, so dass ein geringer Druck für das Modell / den Kunden angenehmer ist. Da das Auftragen der Farbe mit Airbrush mit Gegensatz zum Pinsel oder Schwamm berührungsfrei funktioniert, sollte der Visagist noch behutsamer und vorsichtiger vorgehen, um Augen, Nase und Mund zu meiden. Das Airbrushgerät sollte stets die Nadelschutzkappe tragen, um Verletzungen auszuschließen.

Noch gibt es viele Modelle / Kunden, die noch keine Erfahrung mit dieser Technik haben. Der Visagist sollte sich daher Zeit nehmen, den Kunden / das Modell mit der Technik und dem Luft-/Farbstrahl vertraut zu machen. Bei noch unbekannten Produkten ist ein Probesprühen z.B. am Arm, anzuraten, um mögliche Hautreaktionen zu erkennen. Der Luftstrom sollte immer am Kinn eingesetzt werden, da dieser Bereich unempfindlicher ist. Ein plötzlicher Luftstoß z.B. an den Augen würde den Kunden / das Modell erschrecken.

Bei Airbrush-Make-up-Farben ist auf jeden Fall weniger mehr, denn die Farben sind hochpigmentiert. Jeder Farbauftrag sollte deshalb in dünnen Schichten aufgebaut werden. Sofern Reib- und Wasserfestigkeit des Make-ups gefragt ist, kann die Farbe mit speziellen Make-up Fixierern des jeweiligen Herstellers gefestigt werden.

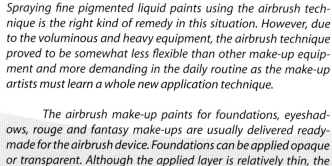

Spraying fine pigmented liquid paints using the airbrush technique is the right kind of remedy in this situation. However, due to the voluminous and heavy equipment, the airbrush technique proved to be somewhat less flexible than other make-up equipment and more demanding in the daily routine as the make-up artists must learn a whole new application technique.

The airbrush make-up paints for foundations, eyeshadows, rouge and fantasy make-ups are usually delivered ready-made for the airbrush device. Foundations can be applied opaque or transparent. Although the applied layer is relatively thin, the high-pigment content spirits away the wrinkles, acne, scars and age spots.

To apply the airbrush make-up, airbrush pistols with a nozzle size of 0,2 mm up to max. 0,5 mm are recommended. Because mostly a single drop of paint is sufficient to cover the face, the gravity-feed system´s colour cup will supply enough paint. The working pressure of the compressor should not exceed 0,7 bar so that the make-up pigments meet the skin in a nearly dry form. Also, the face perceives the air jet stronger than some other parts of the body so that a lower pressure is more welcome by the model / the customer. Compared to a paintbrush or a sponge, the application of the paint with an airbrush device works without direct contact, and that´s why the make-up artist must work with even more caution and care to avoid the eyes, the nose and the mouth. The needle of the airbrush device should always be protected by a cap to eliminate the danger of injury.

There are still many models / customers who have not had any experience with this technique yet. The make-up artist should therefore take enough time to make the model / the customer familiar with the technique and the air and paint jet. If there are some new products at work, it is advisable to test them for example on the arm to find out about the potential skin reactions. The air jet should always be put on in the chin area because it is less sensitive. For example, a sudden air kick in the eyes might scare the customer / the model.

While using the airbrush make-up paints, the rule is that less is more because the paints are highly pigmented. Each paint application should therefore be developed in layers. When rub- and water-resistance is necessary, the paint can be fixated with special make-up fixers.

AUFTRAGEN VON AIRBRUSH-MAKE-UP

APPLICATION OF THE AIRBRUSH MAKE-UP

Für das Auftragen von Airbrush-Make-up gelten hinsichtlich der Farbauswahl, Platzierung und Formgebung die gleichen Regeln wie für die Anwendung von Make-up mit Pinsel und Schwamm. Ihrer Fantasie in Farben, Formen und Accessoires sind daher keine Grenzen gesetzt. Hier zeigen wir Ihnen lediglich das „technische" Auftragen der Foundation sowie eines einfachen Augen- und Wangen-Make-ups mit dem Airbrushgerät. Dies bildet die Grundlage für Ihre eigenen Kreationen.

For the application of the airbrush make-up, the rules concerning the colour choice, positioning and shaping are pretty much the same as the rules of the make-up application with a paintbrush or a sponge. As far as for colours, shapes and accessories, the only limits are the limits of your phantasy. Here we will only show you the "technical" application of the foundation as well as of a simple eye and cheek make-up with an airbrush device. This will be a good foundation for your own creations.

VERWENDETE MATERIALIEN:

- ▶ Airbrush-Fließ-System
- ▶ Airbrush-Make-up-Foundation
- ▶ Airbrush-Make-up: Braun Violett, Pink, Weiß
- ▶ Schmaler Make-up-Pinsel
- ▶ Augenbrauen-, Lid-Schablone

MATERIALS

- ▶ *Airbrush gravity-feed system*
- ▶ *Airbrush make-up foundation*
- ▶ *Airbrush make-up: brown violet, pink, white*
- ▶ *Small make-up paintbrush*
- ▶ *Eyebrow-, eyeshadow-stencil*

STEP 01

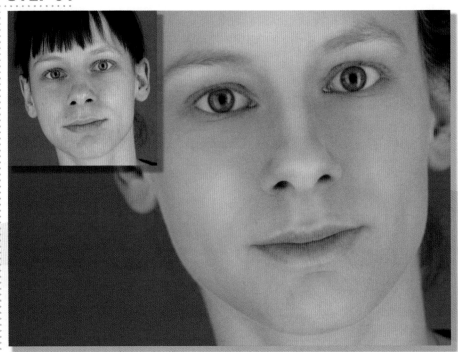

AIRBRUSH-FOUNDATION

Tragen Sie die Foundation in einem Abstand von ca. 10-15 cm und im rechten Winkel zur Haut in kreisenden Bewegungen auf. Beginnen Sie am Kinnbereich. An Detailbereichen wie Nasenflügeln, Augenschatten oder Pickeln arbeiten Sie in einem Abstand von ca. 3-5 cm pulsierend durch eine Hin- und Wegbewegung. Seien Sie sparsam und sprühen Sie nur eine dünne Schicht. Durch die hohe Pigmentierung kommt die Deckung ganz von selbst. Kleine Korrekturen wie der Abschluss am Augenrand können Sie mit einem schmalen Foundationpinsel vornehmen, indem Sie einen Tropfen Make-up aufnehmen, auf die gewünschte Stelle auftragen und ausblenden. Die Foundations sind nach dem Auftrag sofort wischfest und wasserabweisend. In besonderen Fällen wie Hautanomalien, Braut- oder Herren-Make-up können Sie zusätzlich einen Make-up-Fixierer des gleichen Herstellers benutzen. Ein Abpudern ist nicht notwendig.

AIRBRUSH FOUNDATION

Apply the airbrush foundation from a distance of ca 10-15 cm and in a right angle to the skin with rotary movements. Begin in the chin area. In the areas of detail such as the ala of the nose, the dark shadows under the eyes or pickles, work with a distance of 3-5 cm with pulsing back and forth movements. Apply paint sparingly and spray only a thin layer. Due to the high pigment content, the opacity will be provided without any special effort. You can carry out small corrections such as the finish at the edge of the eyes with a small foundation paintbrush in that you take up a drop of the make-up, apply it onto the desired spot and ausblenden. The foundation is smear-resistant and water-repellent immediately after the application. In some special case such as for blemishes, bridal or men´s make-up, you can in addition use a make-up fixation of the same manufacturer. The use of powder is not necessary.

STEP 02

BETONUNG VON AUGENBRAUEN

Legen Sie die Brauenschablone auf den natürlichen Brauenverlauf. Tragen Sie einen grauen oder rauchig braunen Lidschattenton transparent auf, um den Brauen eine natürliche Betonung zu geben.

UNDERSCORING THE EYEBROWS

Place the eyebrow stencil onto the natural eyebrows. Transparently apply a grey or a smoky brown eyeshadow tone to provide for a natural enhancement of the eyebrow.

STEP 03

LIDSCHATTEN

Die Lidschattenschablone legen Sie auf den Wimpernverlauf. Sprühen Sie einen Lidschatten-Ton in einem Abstand von ca. 3 cm im rechten Winkel zum Auge auf die Schablone (!). Der weiche Sprühnebel, der sich auf das Lid legt, reicht für eine sanfte Schattierung vollkommen aus. Setzen Sie zum Schluss unterhalb der Augenbrauen etwas weißen Lidschatten. Durch die Sprühtechnik entstehen sofort weiche Farbverläufe.

EYESHADOWS

Place the eyeshadow stencil onto the eyelashes. Spray an eyeshadow tone from a distance of ca 3 cm in a right angle to the eye onto the stencil (!). The soft overspray which will land on the eyelid is perfectly sufficient for a smooth shading. At the end, apply some white eyeshadow underneath the eyebrows. Thanks to the airbrush technique, soft colour gradations emerge at no effort.

STEP 04

AIRBRUSH-ROUGE

Wählen Sie einen Rougeton. Sprühen Sie diesen auf die Wangenknochen und bei Bedarf auch auf das Augenlid. Ein Ausdruck der Frische entsteht.

FINISH

Mit Mascara, Lippenstift oder Lipgloss, Glitzer-Applikationen o.ä. können Sie dem Airbrush-Make-up je nach Anlass den letzten Schliff geben.

ROUGE

Choose a rouge tone. Spray it on the cheekbones and if required also on the eyelids. An expression of freshness will emerge.

FINISH

Depending upon occasion, you can polish up the whole impression of the make-up with mascara, lipstick or lipgloss, glitter applications etc.

Airbrush Tanning

DAS AIRBRUSH-TANNING, also die Hautbräunung mit Hilfe des Airbrushgerätes, ist im Prinzip eine Weiterentwicklung von Selbstbräunungsanwendungen. Seit vielen Jahren sind Selbstbräunungscremes und -lotionen im Handel erhältlich, die letztlich genauso funktionieren wie das Airbrush-Tanning. Der Unterschied liegt einzig in der Art des Auftragens. Mit dem Airbrushgerät lässt sich die Tanning-Lotion sehr dünn und gleichmäßig aufsprühen. Im Gegensatz zu selbstangewendeten Bräunungscremes gibt es keine ungleichmäßige Farbkonzentration, helle oder dunkle Flecken oder sogar „Farbnasen". Die Tönung kann sehr genau dosiert werden.

THE AIRBRUSH TANNING, it means the tanning of the skin with the help of an airbrush device, is basically an enhancement to the development of self tanning applications. Self tanning creams and lotions, which have been available in trade for years by now, work basically the same way as the airbrush tanning. The only difference is the procedure of application. With the airbrush device, it is possible to spray the tanning lotion very thinly and evenly. Opposite to the self-applied tanning lotions, there is no uneven colour concentration, light or dark stains or even "colour legs". The tanning can be dosed very precisely.

Grundlage von Airbrush-Tanning-Lotions sowie auch handelsüblichen Selbstbräunern ist der Selbstbräunungswirkstoff DHA (Dihydroxyacetone), der aus Zuckerrohr gewonnen wird. DHA ist ein zu 100% natürliches Produkt, das in der Medizin seit mehr als 40 Jahren bekannt und von der amerikanischen FDA-Behörde anerkannt ist. Die Lotionen werden zusätzlich häufig mit Aloe Vera-Extrakten versetzt, die die Haut pflegen und der Lotion einen dezenten Duft verleihen.

The fundament of the airbrush tanning lotions as well as of the in trade available self-tanning is the self tanning agent DHA (dihydroxyacetone) which is extracted from sugar cane. DHA is a 100% natural product known in the medical world for almost 40 years by now and is FDA-approved. The lotion is often added some aloe vera extract for a good skin care and a gentle odour.

DHA reagiert mit den Proteinen der obersten Hautschicht (Epidermis oder Stratum corneum). Es verbindet sich mit den freien Aminosäuren und den Proteinen (Keratin) der Haut und löst die Bräunung als eine natürliche Reaktion aus. Die bräunliche Färbung entsteht nur an der Hautoberfläche. Tiefer liegende Hautschichten und Zellen werden dadurch – anders als durch die UV-A und UV-B-Strahlung von natürlichem Sonnenlicht und Solarium – nicht beeinflusst. So wird auch der natürliche Hautschutzmechanismus (Melanin) nicht beschädigt, wodurch Hautveränderungen (Sommersprossen, Pigmentflecken) entstehen könnten. Daher eignet sich Airbrush-Tanning auch für helle Hauttypen, die zum Sonnenbrand oder Hautveränderungen neigen. Tanning-Lotions sind mit einem unterschiedlichen DHA-Anteil erhältlich, der individuell nach Hauttyp und gewünschter Bräunungstiefe ausgewählt werden sollte. DHA kann in seltenen Fällen Allergien auslösen. Es ist auch möglich, dass Personen überhaupt nicht auf den Wirkstoff DHA (Wahrscheinlichkeit 1:10.000) reagieren. Deshalb sollten Tanning-Lotionen immer erst an einer unauffälligen Körperstelle auf Verträglichkeit getestet werden.

Der Sprayvorgang dauert in etwa 20 Minuten inklusive Vorbereitung und Trocknung. Je nach Lotion kann ein sofortiger oder natürlicher Bräunungseffekt erzielt werden. Klare Tanning-Lotions lösen lediglich den Bräunungsprozess aus, der je nach Lotion und Hauttyp zwischen 2 und 24 Stunden dauert. Getönte Tanning-Lotions legen sofort einen dünnen Farbfilm auf die Haut, um die Dauer des Bräunungsprozesses zu überbrücken. Für den Theater- und Filmbedarf gibt es auch getönte Tanning-Lotions ohne DHA. Diese künstliche Bräune ist nach ihrem Einsatz sofort wieder abwaschbar. Das Auftragen getönter Tanning-Lotions (mit oder ohne DHA) kann für Anfänger zunächst einfacher sein, da das Ergebnis sofort sichtbar und so besser kontrollierbar ist. Bei klarer Lotion müssen Sie kontrollierter arbeiten, da besprühte und freie Stellen nicht unterscheidbar sind.

Das Farbergebnis verbleibt durchschnittlich zwischen 5-10 Tagen auf der Haut. Faktoren wie Hauttyp, Hautzellwechsel, sportliche Aktivität (überhöhtes Schwitzen) sowie auch die verschiedenen Körperstellen beeinflussen die Haltbarkeit. In den ersten Stunden kann es bei getönten Lotionen – ähnlich wie bei zu viel aufgetragenem Make-up – zu einer Abfärbung auf Kleidungsstücke kommen, die sich aber vollständig wieder herauswaschen lassen. Für kontinuierliche Bräunung muss das Tanning wöchentlich erneuert werden.

DHA reacts with the proteins of the outermost skin layer (epidermis or stratum corneum). It bands together with the free amino acids and the proteins (keratin) in the skin and triggers off the tanning as a natural reaction. The brownish tanning only occurs on the surface of the skin. Compared to the UV-A and UV-B radiation of the natural sun light and solarium, the deeper positioned skin layers and cells are not affected so that the natural system of skin protection (melanin) doesn't carry away any damage or skin alteration (freckles, pigment moles). Therefore, airbrush tanning is also suitable for the light skin types which tend to sunburn or to skin alterations. The tanning lotions are available with a different percentage of DHA which should be chosen according to the individual items such as skin type and the desired tan's depth. Sometimes but rarely DHA can cause allergies. It is also possible that some people will not react to the DHA-agents at all (probability 1:10000). Thus, the skin friendliness of the tanning lotions should always and first of all be tested on an unobtrusive spot on the body.

The spraying procedure lasts about 20 minutes including the preparation and drying. Depending on the lotion, there might be an immediate or natural tanning effect. Clear tanning lotions merely trigger off the tanning process which might take – again depending on the skin type and tanning lotion – from 2 to 24 hours. Tanned tanning lotion immediately applies a thin colour film over the skin to bridge the duration of the tanning process. For stage or movie purposes, there are also DHA-free tanning solutions available. The artificial bronzing effect can be washed off after the occasion. At first, the application of the toned tanning lotions (with or without DHA) can be easier for the beginners because the results are immediately visible and so easier to control. The work with the clear tanning lotions is not as easy to control because there is no visible difference between the already sprayed and the still free spots.

The colour results last on the skin for about 5-10 days on average. Items such as skin type, skin cell change, sport activities (excessive sweating) as well as the various body parts influence the durability. Within the first hours, clothes might get coloured up by the toned tanning lotions as it is the case with the oversupply of make-up, but this colouration will entirely wash off. For a continual tanning effect, the tanning must be renewed on a weekly basis.

AUFTRAGEN VON AIRBRUSH-TANNING

1. Einen Tag vor der Anwendung sollte der Kunde / das Modell die Haut enthaaren (wachsen), peelen und mit einer Hautschutzcreme pflegen. Am Tag der Tanning-Anwendung sollte auf Make-up, Lotion, Parfum und Deo verzichtet werden, um die DHA-Wirkung zu gewährleisten und Ungleichmäßigkeiten oder Verfärbungen zu vermeiden. Lange Haare sollten vor dem Tanning hochgebunden werden. Das Tanning sollte in einem gut belüfteten Raum stattfinden. Um Verschmutzungen zu vermeiden, sollte das Modell / der Kunde auf einem Handtuch stehen. Für den professionellen Einsatz sind auch spezielle Tanning-Kabinen mit Luftabsaugung erhältlich.

2. Zum Auftragen des Tannings empfiehlt sich ein Airbrush-Saugsystem mit großer Düse (> 0,5 mm), um in möglichst kurzer Zeit viel Lotion gleichmäßig auf den Körper aufzutragen. Für ein Ganzkörper-Tanning benötigen Sie je nach Körpergröße des Modells/Kunden ca. 60-120 ml Tanning-Lotion. Füllen Sie ausreichend Lotion in den Saugbecher Ihres Gerätes. Verwenden Sie dafür am besten Handschuhe, da die Lotion sonst ggf. dunkle Flecken auf Ihrer Haut hinterlässt.

3. Sprühen Sie die Lotion mit einem Abstand von ca. 20-30 Zentimetern auf den Körper auf. Bearbeiten Sie jeweils Bauch, Rücken, Arme, Beine, Hände, Füße und Gesicht nacheinander. Sprühen Sie dünne Schichten in horizontalen Schwüngen von links nach rechts und zurück auf. Ist die erste Schicht fertig, beginnen Sie eine zweite in vertikalen Schwüngen, um möglicherweise unerreichte Stellen ebenfalls zu bedecken.

4. Beachten Sie vor allem an den Händen, Ellenbogen, Knien, Hals und Po, dass die Haut straff ist und keine Hautfalten entstehen. Dort gelangt sonst keine Lotion hin und es würden „weiße Streifen" entstehen.

5. Besprühen Sie Hände und Füße mit weniger Lotion, da sie die Lotion meist stärker absorbieren und es zu einer verstärkten Bräunung kommt.

APPLICATION OF THE AIRBRUSH TANNING

1. One day before application, the customer / the model should pare off the hair (waxing), peel the skin and apply skin protection cream. On the day of the tanning application, no make-up, lotion, fragrance and deodorant should be used to ensure the effects of DHA and avoid uneven colouration or discolouration. Long hair is to be pinned up before tanning. The tanning should take place in a well ventilated room. To avoid staining, the customer / the model should stand on a towel. For the professional application there are also special tanning booths available.

2. For the application of tanning, the recommended airbrush system is the bottom-feed system with a large nozzle (> 0,5 mm) to be able to apply as much lotion as possible within the shortest time possible. For a whole body tanning and depending on the body size, you will need ca 60-120 ml of the tanning lotion. Load your device with a sufficient amount of lotion. It is the best to use hand gloves for this because the lotion might otherwise leave dark colouration on your skin.

3. Spray the lotion onto the body from ca 20-30 cm distance to the skin. Work successively on the abdomen, back, arms, legs, hands, feet and face. Spray thin layers with horizontal movements from the left to the right and back. Having completed the first layer, you can begin to spray the second one, this time with vertical movements, to hit the spots you might have missed before.

4. Remember that while you are working on the hands, elbows, knees, neck and buttocks, there should be no skin wrinkles and the skin should be stretched tight. Otherwise the lotion can not get into the wrinkles so that there might be „white stripes" left.

5. Spray the hands and the feet with less lotion because usually these areas will absorb more of the lotion and so cause a darker tanning.

PFLEGE-TIPPS NACH DEM TANNING

1. In den ersten Stunden sollte locker sitzende Kleidung getragen werden. Enge Bündchen können die Tanning-Lotion abreiben.

2. Mit dem Duschen oder Baden sollte mindestens 8-12 Stunden nach dem Tanning gewartet werden. Auch das Händewaschen sollte zunächst auf das Notwendigste reduziert werden. Getönte Tanning-Lotions können sich beim ersten Duschen leicht abwaschen. Das ist nur der Farbüberschuss und hat keine Auswirkung auf die Bräunung.

3. Schweißtreibende Situationen direkt nach der Tanning-Anwendung sollten vermieden werden.

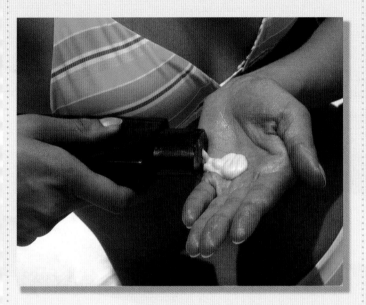

4. Zum Duschen und für die Hautpflege sollten nur öl-, alkohol- und parfumfreie sowie pH-neutrale Produkte verwendet werden. Die Haut sollte täglich mit einer Feuchtigkeitspflege versehen werden, um das Bräunungsergebnis lange zu erhalten. Peeling- und Enthaarungsmaßnahmen sollten vermieden werden.

5. Längere Bäder sowie Schwimmen in Salz- oder Chlorwasser können zum Ausbleichen des Tannings führen und sollten deshalb vermieden werden.

TIPS FOR THE AFTER-TANNING CARE

1. Within the first hours, wear casual clothes. Tight cuffs could rub off the tanning lotion.

2. Wait with taking a shower or having a bath for at least 8-12 hours after the tanning. Also, reduce washing your hands if somehow possible. Toned tanning lotions can wash off slightly with the first shower. However, this is only the lotion oversupply and has no effects on the final tanning.

3. Avoid excessive sweating directly after the application of tanning lotion.

4. To have a shower and take care of the skin, use only oil-free, alcohol-free as well as pH-neutral products. You should use a moisturiser every day for the tanning to last longer. Avoid peeling and depilating.

5. Avoid longer baths as well as swimming in salt or chlorine water. It can cause a bleaching of the tan.

Ganzkörper - Bodypainting
Whole Body Painting

Das Ganzkörper-Bodypainting findet – wie in Kapitel 1 bereits erläutert – überwiegend Anwendung als Eventattraktion, Showpräsentation oder künstlerische Arbeit für Fotoshootings oder Festivalwettbewerbe. Während Airbrush-Tattoos, -Make-up und auch andere Gesichtsschminkanwendungen in der Regel eine Sache von wenigen Minuten sind, brauchen Ganzkörper-Bodypaintings dagegen viel Zeit. Aber auch hier gibt der Anlass den Zeitrahmen vor: Live-Paintings vor Publikum sollten nie länger als 30-60 Minuten dauern, damit dem Publikum nicht langweilig wird. Auch Promotion-Bodypaintings für Messe- und Eventauftritte haben selten länger als zwei bis drei Stunden Zeit. Ausnahmen dagegen bilden die Bodypaintings für die Festival-Wettbewerbe: Hier arbeiten die Künstler sechs bis acht Stunden an ihren Kunstwerken. Besser haben es da jene Künstler, die Bodypaintings als eigene künstlerische Arbeit anfertigen und sich ihre Arbeitszeit selber wählen können. Ganzkörper-Bodypaintings sollten immer gut vorbereitet sein, um das Ergebnis so optimal und die Arbeit für Künstler und Modell so angenehm wie möglich zu gestalten.

The whole body painting is mostly employed – as already mentioned in Chapter 1 – as an event attraction, show presentation or artistic work for photo shootings or festival competitions. While the work on airbrush tattoos, make-up and other face applications usually only takes few minutes, much more time is necessary for the whole body paintings. Nevertheless though, the occasion rules the time frame: live painting in front of an audience should never take longer than 30-60 minutes so that the audience cannot get bored. Similar, the work on promotion body paintings for trade fairs and event performances usually cannot exceed 2-3 hours. And so, the body paintings for the festival competitions constitute an exception: Here the artist can work on their art for 6-8 hours. The artists who create their body paintings in the course of their artistic work and can pick their working times are naturally much better off. Whole body paintings should always be well prepared to allow for an optimal result and also to make the cooperation of the artist and the model as convenient as possible.

MOTIV-VORBEREITUNG

Das Besondere und zugleich die größte Herausforderung des Bodypaintings ist die Form des menschlichen Körpers, seine Lebendigkeit und Bewegungsmöglichkeiten. Diese sollten in die Motivplanung immer einbezogen werden; ansonsten sollte man sich fragen, ob man nicht lieber gleich auf einer Leinwand arbeitet. Daraus folgt, dass sich eine originelle Idee wie ein roter Faden über den Köper ziehen sollte: Keinesfalls eine Aneinanderreihung von kleinen Bildchen, die man nur aus 20 cm Entfernung erkennt, sondern ein Gesamtkunstwerk. Der Betrachter sollte die Idee mit einem Blick erkennen können. Schön ist es, wenn sich dann auch auf den zweiten Blick weitere kleine Details und Nuancen entdecken lassen.

Am besten lassen sich solche Motive anhand von Körperskizzen oder -Fotos konzipieren. Wer die Möglichkeit hat, kann z.B. am Computer vorab Fotomontagen erstellen. Aber auch eine kolorierte Bleistiftskizze des Bodypainting ist eine gute Grundlage. Für einzelne Motive lassen sich dann Fotovorlagen als Referenz verwenden.

Stimmen Sie auch die Wahl der Farben individuell auf Ihr Modell ab. An einem dunklen Typ (mit braunen Augen und/oder dunklen Haaren) wirken warme Farben am besten. Einem hellen Typ (z.B. blond, blaue Augen, helle Haut) stehen kalte Farben am besten. Dies gilt vor allem dann, wenn auch noch einzelne Hautstellen, z.B. im Gesicht, an Armen und Beinen, unbemalt bleiben. Sicherlich bestehen in diesem Punkt nicht immer Wahlmöglichkeiten, insbesondere wenn das Motiv und das Modell von einem Auftraggeber vorgegeben sind. Wenn man dies selbst in der Hand hat, lohnt sich die kritische Auswahl aber in jedem Fall.

PREPARING A MOTIF

The special and at the same time greatest challenge of the body painting is the shape of the human body, its agility and possibility of movement. These factors always should be a part of motif planning; or you might want to ask if you don´t want to paint on canvas right away. Hence, an original idea becomes a leitmotif drawing the attention to the body: It should be no way a sequence of small pictures which you can only see from a 20 cm distance but a complete work of art. The viewers should be able to follow and identify the motif at first glance. However, it is nice when the second glance detects small details and nuances.

It is the best to prearrange the motif with the help of drafts or photos. If you have the possibility, you can for example also create photo montage with a computer. But even a coloured pencil draft of the body painting can deliver a good basis. For the individual motif, you can then use photo samples as a reference.

Also, choose your colours in an individual accordance to your model. Warm colours will work best on a dark type (brown eyes and/or dark hair). The light types (for example blond, blue eyes, light skin) are best served with cold colours. This rule proves its validity especially when there are some spots on the skin (e.g. in the face, on the arms or the legs) that are not to be painted. Certainly, there is not always enough choice in this respect, especially not when the motif and the model are predefined by the customer. However, when all this is in your hand, the critical choosing process is definitely worth your effort.

Ein weiterer Punkt ist die Motiv- und Farbanordnung auf dem Modell: Etwas breitere Hüften sollten nicht unbedingt noch durch helle Farben betont werden, sondern eher mit dunklen Farben etwas zurückgenommen werden.

Kalkulieren Sie die Dauer Ihres Paintings. Am Anfang wird dies sicherlich schwer fallen, aber mit wachsender Erfahrung wird es immer einfacher. Bedenken Sie den Anlass des Paintings, die zur Verfügung stehende Zeit, Ruhepausen für sich und das Modell. Je knapper die Zeit, desto einfacher sollte das Motiv gehalten sein. Zeitmangel sollte nie zu Lasten der Qualität gehen!

Machen Sie sich Gedanken über die Präsentation des Bodypaintings: Braucht Ihr Modell Accessoires, eine bestimmte Frisur? Welcher Hintergrund und welche Pose passt am besten? Stellen Sie ggf. vorher schon passende Hintergründe und Requisiten her. Kümmern Sie sich ggf. um einen Friseur, wenn Sie oder Ihr Modell die Frisur nicht selbst zaubern können. Wie kann und sollte sich Ihr Modell bewegen? Kein Bodypainting kann live oder auf dem Foto gut wirken, wenn das Modell steif und zurückhaltend ist und es an Ausstrahlung fehlt. Stellen Sie vorher sicher, welche Talente Ihr Modell im Posen und Präsentieren, in der Schauspielerei, Tanz oder Akrobatik hat.

Another issue is the motif and colour assembly on the model: There is usually no need to emphasize an already broad beam with light colours but it is possible to reduce it optically with dark colours.

Calculate the duration of your painting. It is certainly going to be difficult in the beginning but the more experience you will gain, the easier it will become. Remember the occasion of the painting, the available time, breaks for you and the model. The less time you have, the simpler you should keep the motif. The lack of time should never be expressed in the lack of quality!

Think about the presentation of the body painting: Does your model need some accessories, a certain hair styling? Which background and which pose are the most suitable? Build the appropriate necessary background and requisites beforehand. Find a hairdresser for your occasion when you cannot conjure up the hairstyling yourself. How should and can your model move? No bodypainting will ever look good live or on the photos if the model is rigid and reluctant and when the charism is missing. Make sure that your model has the necessary talents in the areas of posing, presenting, acting, dancing or acrobatics.

 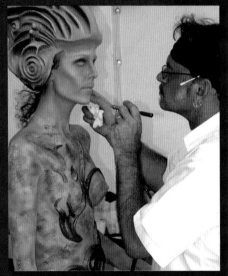 

UMGANG MIT DEM MODELL

Das Ganzkörper-Bodypainting ist aber nicht nur für den Künstler eine Herausforderung, sondern vor allem für das Modell. Bodypainting ist Teamwork. Das Wohlergehen des Modells sollte deshalb immer oberste Priorität haben. Denn ein Modell, das nach mehrstündigem Stillstehen nur noch müde und genervt ist, wird sich bei einer Bühnenpräsentation oder Fotoshooting sicherlich nicht von seiner besten Seite zeigen.

Sprechen Sie vorab das Motiv, den Gestaltungsablauf, die zu erwartende Arbeitsdauer und auch die gewünschte Präsentation mit dem Modell ab, damit es sich darauf einstellen kann. Je besser Sie und das Modell vorbereitet sind, desto reibungsloser läuft das Projekt ab. Teilen Sie dem Modell vorher mit, ob es vor Ort Waschgelegenheiten gibt, damit es sich hinsichtlich Handtuch, Seife oder ggf. älterer Kleidung darauf einstellen kann.

CONTACT WITH THE MODEL

The whole body painting is not only a challenge for the artist but especially for the model. Body painting is teamwork. Therefore, the comfort of the model should always be of highest priority. This is because a model who is tired and annoyed of several hour still-standing will certainly not show its sunny side during the stage presentation or photo shooting.

Agree on the motif, working process, the expected duration as well as the desired presentation with the model beforehand so that she or he can anticipate it. The better prepared you both are, the less problematic you can expect the project to run. Tell the model beforehand if there are washing facilities on the set so that she or he can make arrangements for it – like bringing a towel, soap, or older clothes, if necessary.

BODYPAINTING

Sorgen Sie also dafür, dass sich Ihr Modell wohlfühlt. Viele machen so etwas zum ersten Mal und sind ggf. etwas aufgeregt. Eine gute Atmosphäre und seriöse Umgebung kann also nicht schaden. Seien Sie einfühlsam und geduldig.

Berücksichtigen Sie das ungeschriebene Bodypainting-Gesetz: Bei öffentlichen Bodypaintings sollte das Modell immer einen Slip tragen! Auch wenn Sie und das Modell mit vollkommener Nacktheit kein Problem haben, ist es aus hygienischen Gründen und auch aus Taktgefühl dem Betrachter gegenüber zu vermeiden. Es genügt ein schlichter weißer Slip, ein Tanga oder ein spezieller transparenter Slip aus dem Tanz- und Theaterbedarf. Wenn Sie persönlich für Fotoshootings ein ganz nacktes Modell bevorzugen, dann sollten Sie dies vorher genau mit ihm absprechen.

Verarbeiten Sie nur Farben, die für Bodypainting geeignet sind. Fragen Sie Ihr Modell ggf. nach Allergien oder Hautkrankheiten. Arbeiten Sie außerdem immer mit einem Airbrushgerät mit Nadelschutzkappe. Gerade im Gesicht kann eine offene Nadelspitze gefährlich werden.

After all, make sure that your model feels comfortable. Many of them do such things for the first time and might be somewhat excited. A good atmosphere and a respectful environment can never do any damage. Be emphatic and patient.

Take into consideration the following unwritten law of body painting: At public presentations, the model should always be wearing a slip! Even if you and your model feel free in total nudity, avoid it for hygienic reasons and also out of respect toward the viewers. A simple white slip, a thong underwear or a special transparent slip from the dance and theatre field is good enough! If you personally prefer a totally naked model for your photo shootings, you should definitely agree with the model at this point beforehand.

Work only with paints suitable for body painting. Ask your model about allergies and skin diseases. Also, work with an airbrush device with a needle protection cap. Especially in the face there is a big danger of injury with an open needle.

Geben Sie dem Modell zwischenzeitlich immer wieder Gelegenheit, sich auszuruhen und zu bewegen. Sorgen Sie für ausreichend Getränke, Essen, frische Luft und – wenn möglich – angenehme Temperaturen, damit der Kreislauf stabil bleibt.

Fragen Sie Ihr Modell regelmäßig nach dem Befinden und sprechen Sie zwischenzeitlich die nächsten Schritte ab. Insbesondere wenn Sie an unangenehmen Stellen wie im Gesicht oder den Ohren sprühen, sollten Sie das Modell vorher „warnen". Hier können Sie ggf. auch den Druck am Kompressor etwas herunter regulieren, um den Luftstrahl angenehmer zu machen.

Achten Sie beim Brushen auf Sauberkeit und Ordnung, damit Ihr Modell und auch Sie nicht über Schläuche, Kompressoren und offene Farbflaschen stolpern und Sie alle Materialien schnell und ohne Unterbrechung zur Hand haben.

Arbeiten Sie bei aufwändigen Motiven mit zwei Personen an einem Modell. Sprechen Sie sich in diesem Fall gut ab und achten Sie auf einen gemeinsamen Stil. Sie können die Arbeitszeit so erheblich reduzieren. Manche Arbeiten lassen sich auch mit anderen Techniken, z.B. Pinsel oder Schwamm, durchaus schneller gestalten. Beharren Sie also nicht auf die Airbrush-Technik, wenn anderes sinnvoller wäre.

Always give the model enough opportunity to rest and move. Make sure there is enough to drink, to eat, fresh air and – when possible – comfortable temperature so that the blood circulation remains stable.

Ask your model often if everything is fine and remember to explain the next steps. In particular, when you spray on awkward spots like in the face and around the ears, warn your model at the right time. You can also – if need be – reduce the working pressure of the compressor to make the air jet more acceptable.

Always remember tidiness and order while working with an airbrush so that you and your model cannot stumble upon air hoses, compressors and open paint bottles, and so that you have all materials quickly and readily at your disposal.

Work together with another person on your model when the motif is very demanding. Arrange well for this case and agree on a certain style. This way you can reduce the working time. Some necessary work might be also done much quicker with other means than airbrush, for example paintbrush or a sponge. So, do not stick to the airbrush technique when another one is more reasonable.

MOR STATUE

MARMOREAL STATUE

Die „Marmorierung" des Körpers mit der Airbrush-Technik geht besonders zügig und ergibt recht schnell realistische Effekte. In diesem Step by Step zeigen wir Ihnen den Umgang mit den verschiedenen Airbrush-Systemen sowie das Arbeiten mit losen Schablonen und verschiedenen Sprenkelmethoden. Aber auch das Arbeiten auf einem dunklen Untergrund und das Erzeugen von Strukturen mit dem Airbrushgerät werden demonstriert.

The "marbling" of the body with an airbrush is very quick and results quickly in very realistic effects. In this step by step, we will show you the handling of the different airbrush systems as well as the work with loose stencils and various sprinkling methods. Furthermore, we will demonstrate how to work on a dark ground and produce structures with an airbrush device.

VERWENDETE MATERIALIEN
- ▶ Airbrush-Double-Action-Saugsystem
- ▶ Airbrush-Double-Action-Fließsystem
- ▶ Bodypainting-Farben: Weiß, Schwarz, Blau
- ▶ Mehrere Bögen dickes Papier/Karton
- ▶ Verschiedene Schablonen, Kreisschneider

Materials
- ▶ *Airbrush double-action bottom-feed system*
- ▶ *Airbrush double-action gravity-feed system*
- ▶ *Body painting paints: white, black, blue*
- ▶ *Several sheets of thick paper/cardboard*
- ▶ *Various stencils, circle cutter*

STEP 01

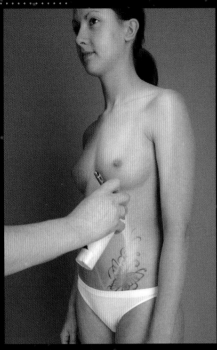

Ein motiviertes Modell ist schon mal die Grundvoraussetzung für ein gutes Bodypainting. Evtl. vorhandene Tattoos werden mit der folgenden weißen Grundierung überdeckt. Das Modell sollte einen hellen Slip tragen, damit dieser später in das Motiv integriert werden kann.

A motivated model is a basic requirement of a good body painting. Potentially existing tattoos will be covered with a white basecoat. The model should be wearing a light-coloured slip so that it can be integrated into the motif later on.

STEP 02

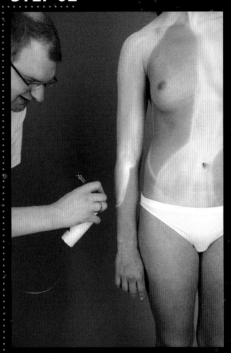

Die Steinstruktur soll nicht am kompletten Körper sein, daher zeichnen Sie als erstes die Bereiche ein, die noch hautfarben bleiben sollen. Sprühen Sie im Abstand von ca. 5 cm zum Körper Linien mit einer Breite von 5 mm – 1 cm auf. Die Form darf ruhig etwas eckig sein, schließlich ist an diesen Stellen der Stein herausgebrochen.

The stone structure should not cover the complete body. Thus, begin with sketching the areas which should keep the skin tone. Spray a line with a width of 5 mm – 1 cm from a distance of ca 5 cm to the body. The shape can be somewhat angled; the stone appears to have broken off on these spots.

STEP 03

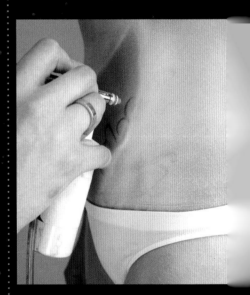

Mit einem größeren Abstand zum Model wird der gesamte Körper mit Weiß in mehreren Schichten grundiert. Sparen Sie dabei die vorher markierten Stellen aus. Sprühen Sie in gleichmäßigen Zügen, damit es zu keinen Fleckenbildungen kommt. Hierbei kommt ein Airbrush Saugsystem zum Einsatz, an das einfach eine große Farbflasche angesteckt wird.

From a bigger distance to the model, create a white whole body basecoat in several layers. Spare the marked areas. Spray with even movements to avoid staining. It is the best to use the bottom-feed airbrush system for this because you only need to clip the bottle.

STEP 04

Nun wechseln Sie die Farbe. Mit Dunkelgrau oder Schwarz sollen viele Sprenkel auf die weiße Fläche gebracht werden, um eine erste Steinstruktur zu gestalten. Für das Sprenkeln gibt es mehrere Möglichkeiten. Besonders schnell funktioniert z.B. die Stöckchen-Methode. Halten Sie das Airbrushgerät in einem 45 Grad Winkel auf einen flachen Stiel (z.B. Eisstiel, Wäscheklammer, altes Cutter-Gehäuse). Drücken Sie dann den Hebel runter und ziehen Sie diesen nach hinten, um Farbe zu versprühen. Die Farbe sammelt sich nun an der Spitze des Stiels und wird mit der weiteren Luft, die ebenfalls austritt, weggepustet. Probieren Sie diese Methode vorher auf einem Bogen Papier aus, bevor Sie evtl. Ihr Motiv durch Sprühnebel zerstören. Sollten Sprenkler auf die freizuhaltenden Körperstellen gelangen, können sie ggf. mit Wasser und einem Tuch entfernt werden.

Now change the colour. With dark grey or black, apply many sprinkles on the white area to develop the first stone structure. There are several possibilities how to create the sprinkles. For example, the stick method is especially quick. Hold the airbrush device in an 45-degree angle onto a flat stick (e.g. stick from an iced-lolly, clothespin, an old cutter body). Then, press down the trigger and pull it back to spray some paint. The paint will gather at the tip of the stick and will be brushed off with the additional air coming from the device. Try to get a hold of this method on a sheet of paper so that you don´t mar your model with overspray. If there are some sprinkles on the body areas which should be kept free, you can remove them with water and a cloth.

STEP 05

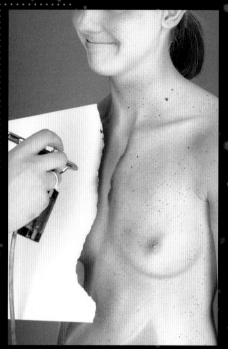

Um die aufgerissenen Kanten der Stein-struktur hervorzuheben, verwenden Sie einen Bogen Karton mit einer abgeris-senen Kante. Legen Sie den Bogen mit der gerissenen Kante an den Übergang von Farb- und Hautton und sprühen Sie vorsichtig mit Schwarz an der Kante ent-lang. So können Sie den ganzen Bereich deutlich farbig absetzen.

To underscore the broken edges of the stone structure, use a sheet of a cardboard with a torn edge. Place the cardboard with the torn edge onto the border between the skin and the colour tone and carefully spray along the edge with black. This will clearly contrast the two areas.

STEP 06

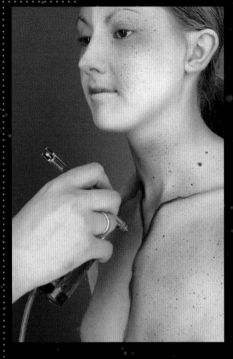

Im nächsten Schritt arbeiten Sie die Kanten freihand weiter aus. Um einen Riss zu simulieren, sprühen Sie ganz dicht am Körper eine feine, gezitterte Linie auf. Sie können diese Risse direkt von einer Kante aus starten oder auch an anderen passenden Stellen einbauen. Nutzen Sie dabei auch die natürliche Körperform und ziehen Sie z.B. Risse am Schlüsselbein entlang oder von der Achsel ausgehend. Auch den Slip können Sie natürlich mit einarbeiten.

The next step is to work out the edge freehand. To simulate a crack, spray a fine shaky line from very closely to the body. You can let these cracks start directly at the edge or build them in on different spots. Watch the natural body shape and use it for your benefit in that you e.g. create the cracks on spots such as along the wishbone or the armpits. You can of course integrate the slip into the cracks too.

STEP 07

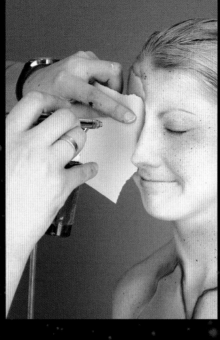

Auch im Gesicht werden die Steinkanten mit einer losen gerissenen Schablone gesprüht. Achten Sie hierbei darauf, ganz vorsichtig und behutsam vorzugehen, damit das Modell keine Farbe oder Papierecken in die Augen bekommt. Drosseln Sie den Druck auf etwa 0,5-1 bar herunter, wenn Sie im Gesicht arbeiten.

Also in the face, the stone edges will be created with a loose torn stencil. Remember to work very carefully and with caution to avoid spraying paint into the model´s eyes or hurting the eyes with paper. Reduce the pressure to 0,5-1 bar when you are working on the face.

STEP 08

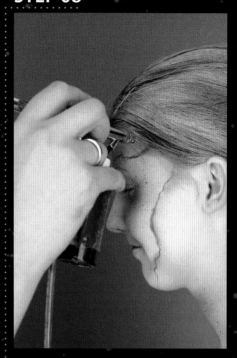

Gezitterte Linien und Risse setzen auch im Gesicht und auf den Haaren die Struktur fort. Um das Modell nicht zu verletzen, ist es ratsam, im Gesicht mit einer Nadelschutzkappe am Gerät zu arbeiten.

Shaky lines and cracks continue the structure also in the face and in the hair. To avoid hurting the model, you should work with a needle protection cap while working on the face.

MARMORSTATUE

STEP 09

STEP 10

STEP 11

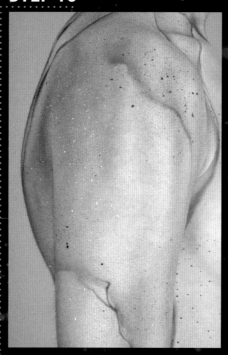

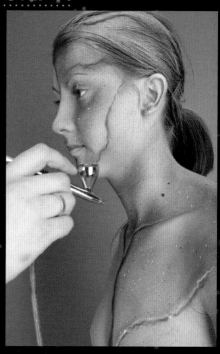

Sprühen Sie jetzt mit Schwarz und grö-ßerem Abstand am ganzen Körper ein wenig Farbe auf, um die Grundierung leicht grau einzufärben. Die Schattie-rung darf wie in der Natur auch gerne unregelmäßig und leicht fleckig sein.

Neben den schwarzen Sprenkel wer-den nun auch noch weiße Sprenkel auf den ganzen Körper gespritzt. Diesmal kommt die Schlauchabknick-Metho-de zum Einsatz: Dazu knicken Sie den Schlauch ab und drücken den Airbrush-hebel von vorn nach hinten durch. Um immer ein wenig Luft zum Sprenkeln in das Gerät zu lassen, öffnen und schlie-ßen Sie den Schlauchknick durch Pum-pen (siehe Seite 50).

Die Risse sollen nun noch eine Lichtkan-te bekommen. Sprühen Sie parallel zur schwarzen, gezitterten Linie noch eine weiße daneben. Dieser Kontrast ver-stärkt die Plastizität der Struktur.

Spray black from a somewhat bigger dis-tance onto the whole body to colour the basecoat light grey. The shading can look naturally uneven and stained.

Having finished the black sprinkles, spray the whole body with white sprinkles. This time, use the squeeze method: Squeeze the hose and press the airbrush trigger all the way back. To let some air into the airbrush device for sprinkling, open and close the hose squeeze with pumping (see page 50).

The cracks should also gain a light edge. Spray a white line next to the black shaky one to boost the contrast and the plasticity of the structure.

STEP 12

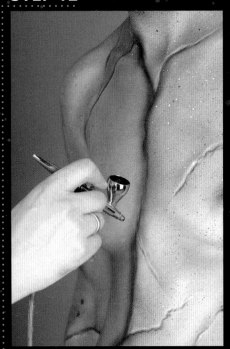

Damit sich die freigelegte Körperstelle von der Steinstruktur noch etwas mehr abhebt, haben Sie die Möglichkeit, an dieser Stelle noch einen Schattenwurf einzusprühen. Arbeiten Sie vorsichtig mit etwas Schwarz an der Innenkante entlang, um den weichen Schatten zu simulieren.

To counterpoint the free body spots and the stone structure even more, you can also spray shadows on these spots. Work carefully with some black paint along the inner edge to simulate a soft shadow.

STEP 13

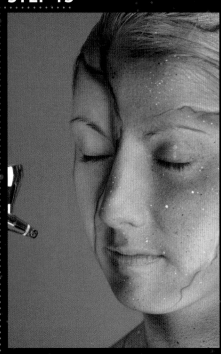

Auch im Gesicht sprühen Sie vorsichtig die Schattierung an der Kante entlang. Das „Loch" erhält dadurch mehr Tiefe.

Carefully spray some shadings also along the edges in the face. Thanks to this, the "hole" will gain more depth.

STEP 14

Hier sehen Sie den Zwischenstand – damit ist die Steinstruktur abgeschlossen. Je nachdem, welches Endresultat man erreichen möchte, kann man dies natürlich auch so stehen lassen. Die Steinstruktur ist für den Betrachter allein schon ein interessantes Motiv. Die Struktur lässt sich sowohl komplett am ganzen Körper wie eine Statue als auch z.B. nur im Gesicht oder – wie hier - mit „Lücken" gestalten.

You can see the preliminary result here – the stone structure is complete now. Depending upon the desired final result, you can leave the motif as it is at this point. The stone structure is an interesting motif on itself for many viewers. The structure can be designed on the complete body as to create a statue but also e.g. only in the face or – with "gaps".

MARMORSTATUE

STEP 15

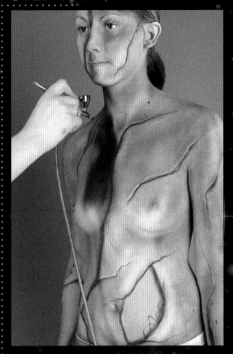

STEP 16

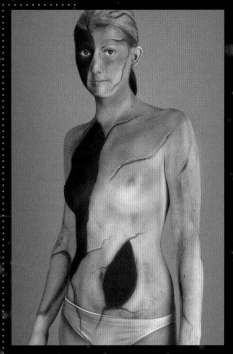

STEP 17

In den Aufrisslöchern sollen jetzt noch andere Motive hindurchblitzen. Hierbei sind unzählige Variationen denkbar – durchwachsende Pflanzen, menschliches Gewebe und Organe, Unterwasser-Landschaften u.v.m. In diesem Beispiel soll eine Weltraum-Kulisse durch die Steinumhüllung schauen. Dazu ist es zunächst einmal notwendig, die noch freien Flächen mit Schwarz zu grundieren. Da die Flächen nicht all zu groß sind, können Sie auch mit einem Airbrush-Fließsystem arbeiten.

Hier sehen Sie die ausgemalten Flächen und den höheren Kontrast zu der nun recht hell wirkenden Steinstruktur.

Mit einem Kreisschneider schneiden Sie aus einer Pappe einen großen Kreis aus. Die Pappe dient als lose Maskierung für den ersten Planeten. Legen Sie die Schablone an und sprühen Sie mit Weiß als erstes die Lichtkante des Planeten ein. Das geht am besten mit einem Abstand von 5-10 cm. Achten Sie darauf, dass nur oben links die Lichtkante eingenebelt und nicht am ganzen Kreis entlang gesprüht wird.

At the gaps where the stones were torn off, some other motifs should leap out. Only the imagination sets borders to the endless variations – among others e.g. intermingled plants, human tissues or organs, underwater landscapes. In this example, a space coulisse penetrates the stone webbing. First of all it is necessary to apply a black basecoat to the still free areas. Because these areas are not very large, you can also work with a gravity-feed airbrush system.

Here you can see the painted areas and the sharper contrast to the stone structure which now appears very light.

Use a circle cutter to cut a large circle out of a cardboard. This cardboard provides for a loose masking to create the first planet. Place the stencil into position and first of all spray white to create a light edge of the planet. It is the best to keep a distance of about 5-10 cm to the body. Remember that the light edge should only be spray at the left top and not along the whole circle.

STEP 18

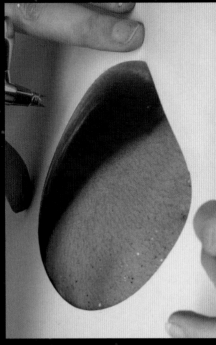

Um ein wenig Planetenoberfläche bzw. Atmosphäre anzudeuten, sprühen Sie an der Rundung entlang einige gezitterte Linien auf.

To indicate some surface or respectively an atmosphere of the planet, spray some shaky lines along the rounding.

STEP 19

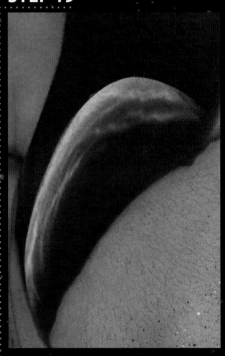

Zum Planenteninneren hin entsteht ein abnehmender Farbverlauf. Die gezitterten Linien werden etwas breiter, damit der Planet nur sichelförmig dargestellt ist.

There is a colour gradient diminishing toward the inner of the planet. The shaky lines are somewhat wider and the planet appears crescent-shaped.

STEP 20

Mit einer weiteren Kreisschablone wird ein kleinerer Planet am Oberkörper eingesprüht. Starten Sie dabei wieder mit einer Lichtkante. Anschließend sprühen Sie als Strukturgebung dünne gezitterte Linien von links nach rechts auslaufend ein.

With another circle stencil, spray a smaller planet on the upper body. Begin again with a light edge. Subsequently, spray thin shaky lines fading out from the left to the right side to provide some structure.

MARMORSTATUE

STEP 21

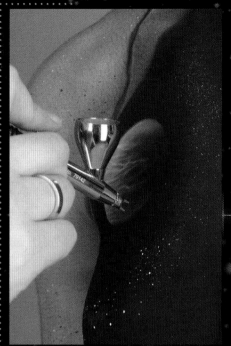

STEP 22

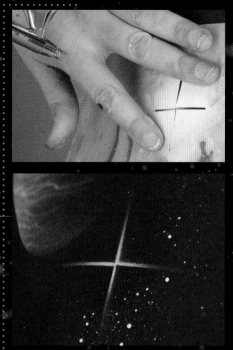

STEP 23

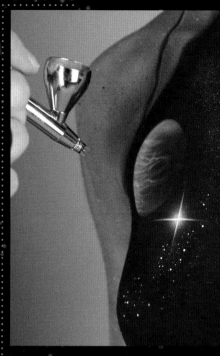

Für weit entfernte Galaxien und Sterne eignet sich wieder die Schlauchabknickmethode. Sprenkeln Sie einige Milchstraßen und Sterne mit Weiß in den schwarzen Bereich hinein.

Zur weiteren Unterstreichung wird ein funkelnder Stern in den Weltraum gebrusht. Dazu benutzen Sie eine lose Stern-Schablone, für die Sie aus Papier oder Karton zwei ganz dünne gekreuzte Rechtecke mit einem Durchmesser von ca. 1 x 50 mm ausschneiden. Drücken Sie die Kreuz-Maskierung gut am Körper an und sprühen Sie nun ganz vorsichtig nur in die Mitte ein wenig Weiß. Auf keinen Fall komplett ausmalen, da die Farbe sich ja automatisch in den Balken durch den Sprühkegel verstreuen soll. (vgl. Seite 51).

Nehmen Sie anschließend die Maskierung herunter und sprühen Sie mit einem Abstand von 5 bis 8 cm in die Mitte einen Sprühpunkt ein. Jetzt beginnt der Stern richtig zu leuchten!

For the distant galaxies and stars, the squeeze method is very suitable. Sprinkle some milky ways and stars with white into the black areas.

To visually bring the space out even more, brush a twinkling star. For this, use a loose stencil which you get when you cut two very thin, crossed rectangles with a dimension of 1 x 50 mm out of a paper or a cardboard. Press the cross masking onto the body and spray very carefully some white into its middle. Do not completely paint it because the paint should scatter across the arms as you simply spray the jet (see page 51).

Subsequently, remove the masking and spray a dot into the middle from a distance of 5 to 8 cm. Now the star truly begins to twinkle!

STEP 24

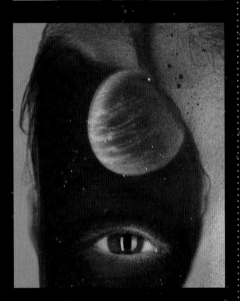

Für weitere Planeten im Kopfbereich können Sie entweder wieder mit dem Kreisschneider einen kleineren Kreis schneiden oder Sie greifen auf eine fertige Kreisschablone (im Handel erhältlich) zurück.

For the other planets in the head area, you can either cut out a smaller circle with a circle cutter or you can grab a ready-made circle stencil (available in trade).

STEP 25

Hier sehen Sie den bisherigen Zwischenstand. An einigen Stellen wurden noch Sprühpunkte auf die Sprenkel gesetzt, damit auch diese Sterne erleuchten.

You can see the preliminary result right here. On some spots, spray dots were brushed onto the sprinkles to make these stars also twinkle.

STEP 26

Mit Blau erhalten die Planeten nun noch ein wenig Farbe. Dabei ist es wichtig dass Sie eine transparente Farbe benutzen, die kein Weiß enthält. Der Planet hat seine Formgebung und Struktur mit Weiß erhalten und wird durch das Blau leicht eingefärbt, aber nicht abgedeckt. Wenige Sprühstöße reichen aus, um die Planeten leicht einzufärben. Das Blau wird nur auf den weißen Strukturen sichtbar und von der schwarzen Umgebung geschluckt.

The planets will obtain colour when you use some blue paint. Now it is important to use a transparent paint with no white contents. The planet received its structure through white and should be lightly coloured but not covered with blue. Few spray blows are sufficient to colour up the planets. The blue will be visible on the white structures but swallowed by the black surroundings.

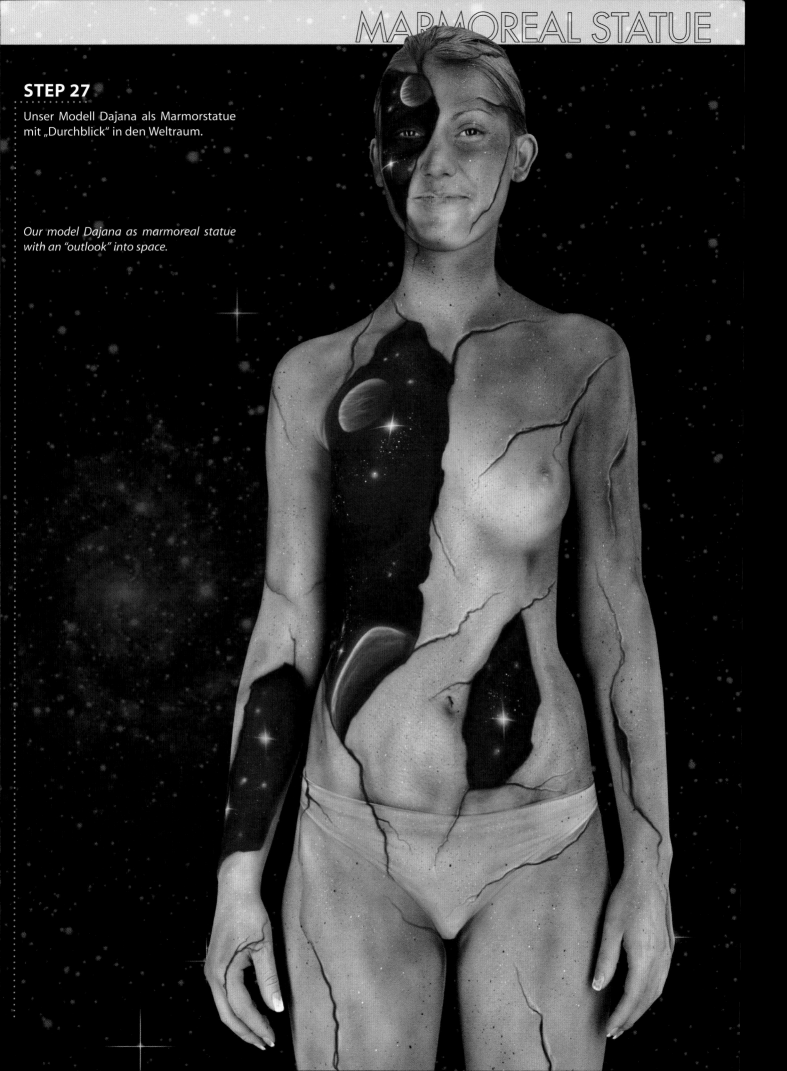

STEP 27

Unser Modell Dajana als Marmorstatue mit „Durchblick" in den Weltraum.

Our model Dajana as marmoreal statue with "outlook" into space.

LEO

VERWENDETE MATERIALIEN

- ▷ Airbrush-Double-Action-Saugsystem
- ▷ Airbrush-Double-Action-Fließsystem
- ▷ Bodypainting-Farben: Weiß, Hellbeige, Braun, Gelb, Schwarz
- ▷ Nail Art-Schablone
- ▷ Airbrush-Acryl-Farbe: Weiß, Schwarz, Gelb

MATERIALS

- ▷ Airbrush double-action bottom-feed system
- ▷ Airbrush double-action gravity-feed system
- ▷ Body painting paints: white, light beige, brown, yellow, black
- ▷ Nail art stencil
- ▷ Airbrush acrylic paints: white, black, yellow

LEOPARD

PARD

Bei unserem nächsten Motiv wird das Modell zum Raubtier. Der Leoparden-Look wird nahezu komplett frei-hand gesprüht. Ein wenig Erfahrung mit dem Airbrushgerät ist dabei natürlich nötig, damit die Farbe nicht vom Körper tropft. Grundsätzlich sind solche „tierischen" Strukturen wie Leopardenmuster, Tiger- und Zebrastreifen für den Betrachter immer sehr eindrucksvoll und für den Bodypainting-Einsteiger leicht umzusetzen. Kombiniert wurde das Bodypainting mit einer einfachen Fingernagelbemalung, bei der ebenfalls die Airbrush-Technik ein-gesetzt wurde.

In the course of the our next motif, the model becomes a predator. The leopard-look will be applied almost entirely free-hand. Some experience with the airbrush device is naturally necessary so that the paint does not trickle from the body. On principle, such animal motifs as the leopard pat-tern, tiger or zebra stripes are very impressive for the viewer and easy to design for the body painting beginner. This body painting is combined with a simple nail paint which was also created with the airbrush technique.

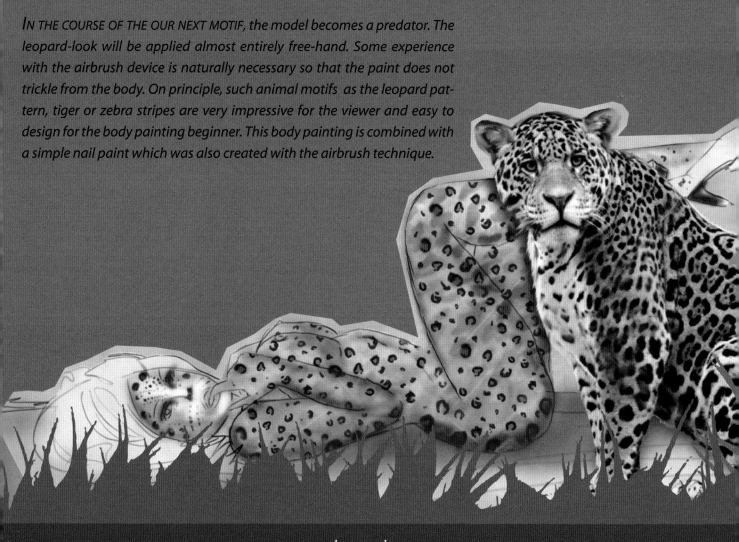

STEP 01

Starten Sie wieder mit einer Grundierung aus Weiß. Das Weiß muss nicht hundertprozentig deckend sein, da anschließend noch Brauntöne aufgesprüht werden, die ebenfalls Weiß enthalten und somit zusätzlich Deckkraft haben. Dennoch unterstützt eine weiße Grundierung bei vielen Motiven zusätzlich die Leuchtkraft der Farben.

Begin again with a white basecoat. The white paint doesn't need to be 100% opaque because brown tones will be sprayed over it later. These too contain white and with it additional opacity. Nevertheless, the white basecoat means additional colour luminance for many motifs.

STEP 02

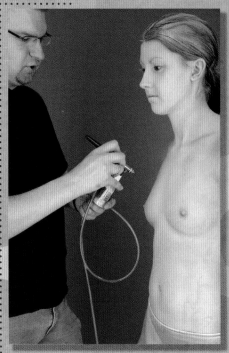

Mischen Sie aus Braun, Weiß und evtl. etwas Gelb einen hellen Beige-Farbton. Sprühen Sie mit dieser Farbe einen Streifen zentriert am Körper herunter. Starten Sie am Kopf, dann über den Hals, Brustkorb und Bauch. Sprühen Sie diese Farbe auch an den Innenschenkeln entlang.

Mix brown, white and possibly some yellow into a light beige tone. With this colour, spray a downward stripe centrally onto the body. Begin with the head, then the neck, the chest and the belly. Spray this colour also along the inner shanks.

STEP 03

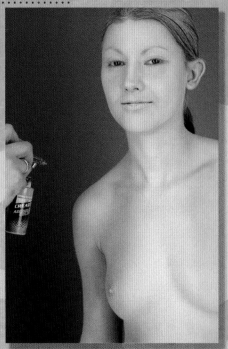

Jetzt geht es weiter mit einem Braun-Orange-Gemisch. Links und rechts vom mittleren Streifen aus sprühen Sie mit dieser Farbe die weitere Fläche des Körpers nach außen hin aus. Damit alles gleichmäßig und ohne Flecken aufgetragen wird, sprühen Sie in gleichmäßigen Zügen die Farbe auf.

Now you get on with the brown-orange mix. Spray this colour on the wider area of the body on the left and right side of the central stripe with a outward movement. To make sure everything is applied evenly and without stains, spray the paint with even movements.

LEOPARD

STEP 04

STEP 05

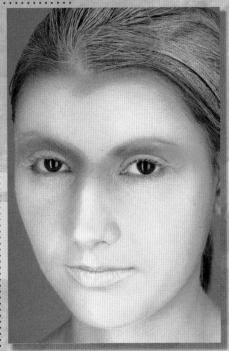

STEP 06

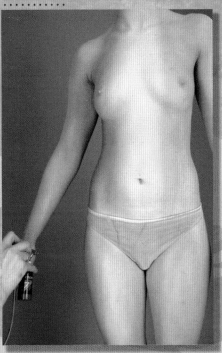

Im Gesicht nutzen Sie diese Farbe, um eine erste Motiv-Struktur vorzubereiten. Sprühen Sie vorsichtig oberhalb der Stirn, über die geschlossenen Augen und das Nasenbein, über die Ohren und Wangen bis zum Kinn hinab. Es sollte eine weiche Farbabstufung zur weißen Grundierung entstehen. Achten Sie darauf, dass noch etwas Weiß im Gesicht erhalten bleibt, um später einen interessanten Kontrast für die Flecken zu erhalten.

Mit Braun werden die Farbübergänge nach außen hin noch etwas abgedunkelt. Auch der Lidschatten wird damit kräftiger.

Ebenfalls mit Braun dunkeln Sie die Farbverläufe am restlichen Körper ab.

Use this colour in the face to prepare for the first motif structure. Spray carefully above the forehead, over the closed eyes and the nasal bone, over the ears and cheeks down to the chin. You should create a soft gradation to the white basecoat. Remember to leave some white in the face to obtain an interesting contrast for the spots later on.

Darken up the colour transitions with brown. This also strengthens the eyeshadows.

Darken up the rest of the colour transitions on the body with this brown.

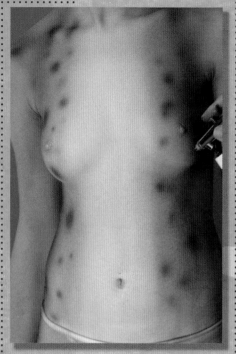

Die Grundlage für die Leopardenflecken bilden braune Punkte und Flecken. Später kommt dann jeweils ein schwarzer Fleck darüber. Sprühen Sie nach außen etwas größere Flecken und nach innen hin etwas kleinere Punkte. Achten Sie darauf, dass die Punkte nicht zu symmetrisch nebeneinander liegen und nicht alle die gleiche Größe haben.

The fundament for the leopard´s rosettes are brown spots and stains. Later, a black stain will be applied. Spray the bigger stains outwards and some smaller spots inwards. Remember that the rosettes are not a far too symmetrical pattern and that they are not all of the same size.

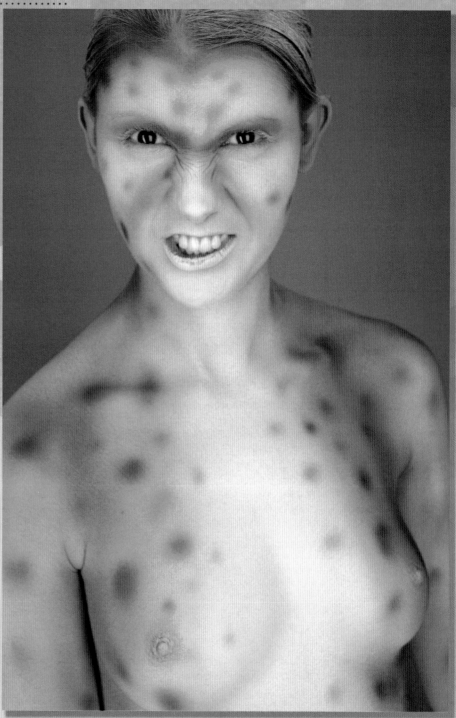

Auch im Gesicht werden einige braune Grundierungsflecken gesprüht.

Spray some brown basecoat spots also in the face.

LEOPARD

STEP 09

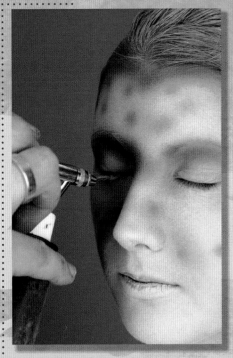

Mit Schwarz werden ganz vorsichtig die Augenbrauen noch etwas abgedunkelt.

Carefully darken up the eyebrows with black.

STEP 10

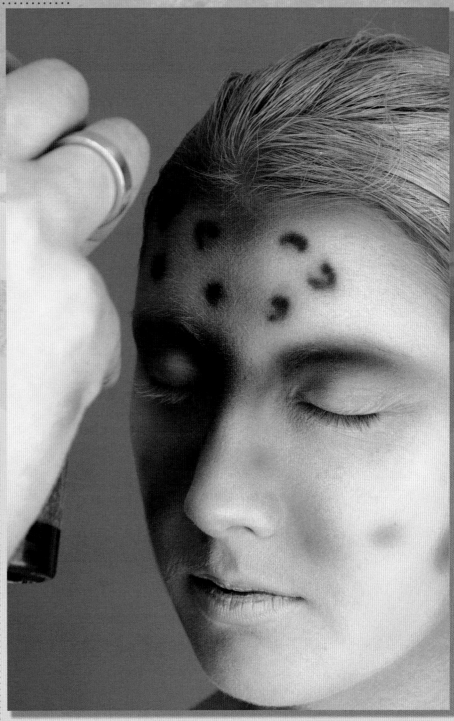

Sprühen Sie nun die typischen Leopardenflecken mit Schwarz auf. Einige sind etwas hufeisenförmig, andere kleinere Flecken sind nur Sprühpunkte. Benutzen Sie die vorher aufgesprühten braunen Flecken als Grundlage und lassen Sie diese zentriert durchschauen. Schauen Sie sich als Hilfestellung zuvor ein Foto eines Leoparden an, um eine genauere Vorstellung von dem Muster zu bekommen.

Spray the typical leopard rosettes with black. Some are somewhat horseshoe-shaped, some other small rosettes are just sprayed dots. Use the beforehand-sprayed brown stains as a basis and let them stand out centrally. Before you work on this, make sure you have a photo of a leopard at hand to assist you clearing up the idea of the leopard pattern.

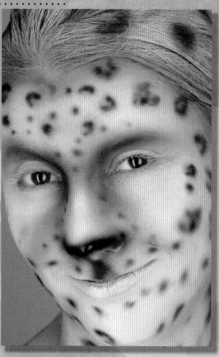

Jetzt geht es nochmal weiter im Gesicht. Sprühen Sie mit Schwarz besonders vorsichtig den unteren Bereich der Nase an. Zwischen Oberlippe und Nase ebenfalls ein wenig, um die Schnauze des Leoparden anzudeuten.

Let's get on with some work in the face. Spray especially carefully the lower area of the nose black. Apply some of it also between the nose and the upper lip to indicate the mouth of the leopard.

Hier sehen Sie den Zwischenstand. Einige große Leopardenflecken haben noch einen Sprühpunkt in die Mitte bekommen. Sprühen Sie die Fleckenstruktur auch in die Haare, um das gesamte Erscheinungsbild abzurunden.

Here you can see the preliminary result. Some large leopard rosettes have now a spray dot in the middle. Spray the rosette pattern also into the hair to top off the complete appearance.

LEOPARD

STEP 13

Hier können Sie gut sehen, wie ein wenig mehr Farbe den Ausdruck im Gesicht verändert. Optional können Sie auch unter die Unterlippe ein wenig Schwarz sprühen, um den Mund noch ein wenig zu betonen.

Here you can see very well how a little more of some colour can change the facial expression. There is an open option to spray a bit of black also underneath the lower lip to underscore the mouth even more.

STEP 14

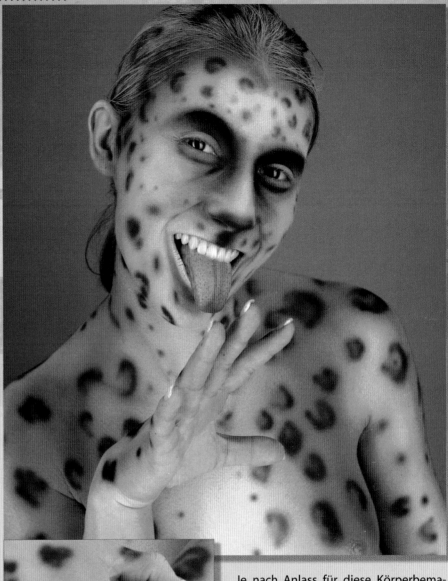

Je nach Anlass für diese Körperbemalung sprühen Sie die Leopardenstruktur auch auf den ganzen Körper, d.h. auch die Unterarme und den Rücken nicht zu vergessen. Als krönenden Abschluss können Sie mit einer einfachen Nail Art-Schablone auch die Fingernägel mit einem Leoparden-Muster verzieren. Sprühen Sie mit einer Airbrush-Acryl-Farbe erst eine weiße Grundierung auf die Nägel, danach eine Schicht Gelb. Wenn die Grundierung gut getrocknet ist, legen Sie die Nail Art-Schablone auf und sprühen mit Schwarz an jedem Finger das Muster auf.

Depending on the occasion of this body painting, you can spray the leopard pattern onto the whole body, i.g. you should not forget the forearms and the back. As a grand finale, you can decorate the finger nails with the leopard pattern using a simple nail stencil. First of all, spray a white basecoat onto the nails with an airbrush acrylic paint. Now a yellow layer can follow. When the basecoat has dried properly, place the nail art stencil onto the nails and spray the pattern on each finger with black.

Von einem anderen Stern kommt das Alien Girl. Mit den in den Grundlagen erlernten Schuppenstrukturen können Sie interessante Effekte auf dem Körper erzielen. Kombiniert mit Schablonen kommen Sie schnell zum gewünschten Ergebnis und können den menschlichen Körper ruck zuck in ein fremdartiges Wesen verwandeln.

The Alien Girl comes from a different star. You can obtain interesting effects on the body with the basics explained in the previous chapters. Combining these with the stencils, you can quickly come up with the desired result and turn the human body into an outlandish creature.

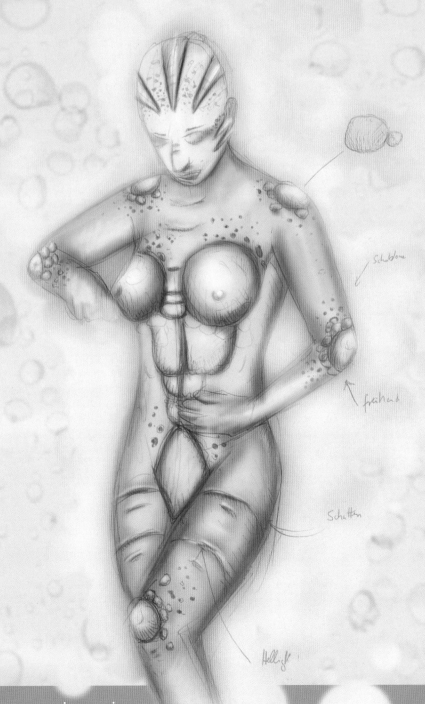

VERWENDETE MATERIALIEN

- Airbrush-Double-Action-Saugsystem
- Bodypainting-Farben: Weiß, Dunkelgrün, Hellgrün, Gelb, Schwarz
- Special-Effects-Schablonen

MATERIALS

- *Airbrush double-action bottom-feed system*
- *Body painting paints: white, dark green, light green, yellow, black*
- *Special effects stencils*

STEP 01

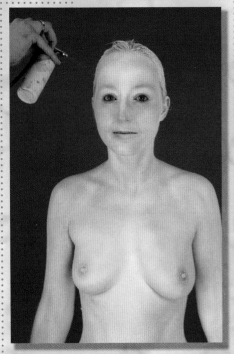

Bei diesem Bodypainting habe ich mich für eine grüne Grundfarbe entschieden. Andere Farben wie Blau oder Rot sind ebenfalls sehr eindrucksvoll und können von Ihnen beliebig getauscht werden. Damit die Farben gut leuchten, ist eine weiße Grundierung ratsam. Unser Modell hat sehr lange Haare, daher wurden diese zusammengebunden. Die entstehende glatte Haarfläche kann dann sehr gut in das Bodypainting eingearbeitet werden.

I decided to use a green base colour. Other colours such as blue or red are also very impressive and you can swap them at your heart´s wish. A white basecoat is advisable to make the colours brighter. Our model had very long hair which is why we decided to pin it up. The created smooth hair surface can be easily integrated into the body painting.

STEP 02

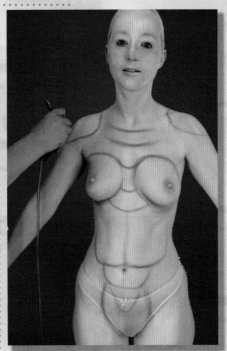

Zur Orientierung werden die ersten Linien und Formen auf den Körper gesprüht. Verwenden Sie dazu Dunkelgrün. Auf den Schultergelenken brushen Sie ein kreisförmiges Muster – später werden daraus Schuppenplatten. Sprühen Sie ebenfalls die Linien für die Bauchmuskeln und die Betonung der Brust.

To establish a rough planning, spray some initial lines and shapes onto the body using dark green. Brush a circle-shaped pattern onto the shoulder joints – these will later become scale plates. Spray also the lines for the belly muscles and accentuate the chest.

STEP 03

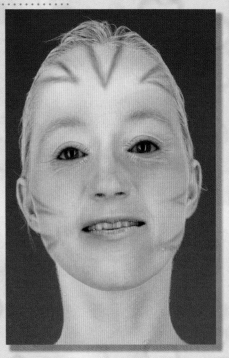

Auch das Gesicht bekommt einige Linien. Sprühen Sie im oberen Kopfbereich drei Keile und an den Wangen jeweils noch zwei.

The face also gets some lines. Spray three wedges in the upper head area and two on each cheek.

ALIEN GIRL

STEP 04

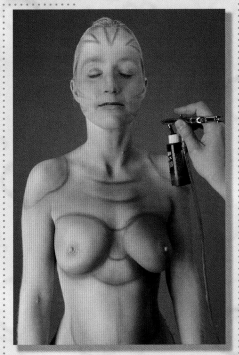

Sprühen Sie jetzt mit einem helleren Grün (also mit mehr Gelbanteil) die Formen aus. Grundsätzlich könnten Sie den ganzen Körper nun mit diesem Farbton übernebeln – lassen Sie aber einige helle Lichtbereiche etwas frei. Beginnen Sie am besten jeweils an den dunklen Linien und arbeiten Sie von dort aus im Verlauf in die hellen Bereiche.

Spray the shapes with a light green (it means with a bigger portion of yellow). You could basically overspray the whole body with this colour tone – but it is better you leave some light areas somewhat free of it. It is the best to begin with the dark lines and go from here in gradients into the lighter areas.

STEP 05

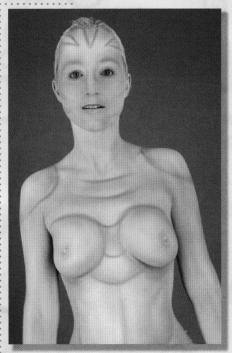

Füllen Sie jetzt die hellen Bereiche mit Gelb aus. Sie sehen, wie in den jeweiligen Körperregionen die Schattierungen von der dunklen Kante über Grün bis Hellgrün übergehen. Durch diese Schattierungen können Sie den Alien-Körperbau etwas dreidimensionaler gestalten und die Formgebung betonen.

Fill the light areas with yellow. Now you can see how the shading in each body area is graduating from the dark edge into green and finally light green. Thanks to this shading, you can design the alien body somewhat three-dimensional and underscore the shapes.

STEP 06

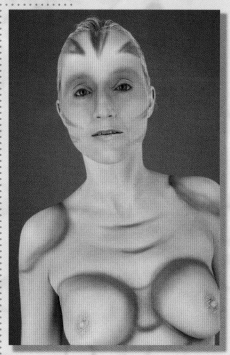

Mit Dunkelgrün geht es nun weiter. Von den Konturen ausgehend sprühen Sie an den Schulterplatten und den Brüsten jeweils eine dunkle Schattierung auf. Auch die Keile oben am Kopf werden noch einmal betont. Sprühen Sie außerdem das Dunkelgrün in den Augenhöhlen und an der Nase entlang. Gehen Sie an diesen sensiblen Stellen behutsam vor und sprechen Sie mit dem Modell immer die nächsten Schritte ab.

Let´s get on with some dark green. Beginning with the contours, spray a dark shadow on each shoulder plate and on the chest. Also, you will again accentuate the wedges on the upper head. Spray the dark green also into the eyeholes and along the nose. Proceed on these spots very carefully and always talk to the model about the next steps.

STEP 07

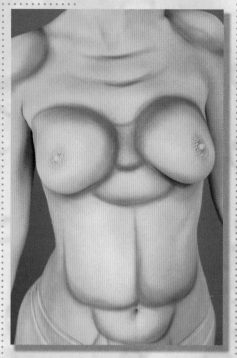

Sprühen Sie ebenfalls noch ein wenig Schatten im Bereich der Bauchmuskeln. Durch den Abstand zum Malgrund haben Sie die Möglichkeit, wenig oder viel Farbe aufzutragen und können damit die Intensität der Farbe steuern. Sie können einen weichen Übergang von der dunklen Kante zur hellgrünen Grundfarbigkeit erreichen.

Spray some shadings also in the area of the belly muscles. Through the varying distance to the working surface, you are able to apply a lot or just a little bit of paint and so to control the intensity of the colour. You can obtain a soft gradiation from the dark edge to the light green base colour.

STEP 08

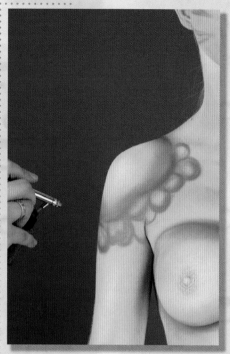

An den Schulterplatten werden jetzt rundliche Schuppenelemente hinzugefügt. Starten Sie mit der Umrandung und sprühen Sie dann im nächsten Arbeitsgang zusätzlich die Schattierung der Schuppen ein, indem Sie von der Umrandung aus einen leichten Verlauf zur jeweiligen Kreismitte anlegen.

On the shoulder plates, add now the roundish scales-like elements. Begin again with their edges and spray the shading of the scaling in the next work step. Create a light gradient toward the middle of each circle.

STEP 09

Mit Hilfe einer Make-up-Schablone werden weitere kleine Schuppenstrukturen ergänzt. Legen Sie die Schablone unterhalb der Kreisformen an und sprühen Sie sie transparent mit dem dunklen Grünton aus. Alternativ können Sie auch aus Karton bzw. stärkerem Papier und mit einem Cutter ähnliche Muster ausschneiden und so eine eigene Schablone herstellen. Das Ergebnis ist das gleiche.

With the help of a make-up stencil, create additional small scaling structures. Place the stencil underneath the circle shapes and spray them with the transparent dark green. You can also cut similar patterns out of cardboard or respectively a thicker paper with a cutter and create your own stencil. The result will be the same.

ALIEN GIRL

STEP 10

STEP 11

Mit einer weiteren Schablone sprühen Sie noch feinere Strukturen auf. Zum Brustkorb hin werden die Strukturen immer kleiner.

Spray some even finer structures with another stencil. The structures are getting smaller and diminishing toward the chest.

Hier sehen Sie, wie die Maskierung vorsichtig abgehoben und das Muster sichtbar wird. Später wird es noch überarbeitet und freihand verstärkt.

Here you can see the masking being carefully removed and the pattern becoming visible. Later you will work on this again and accentuate everything free-hand.

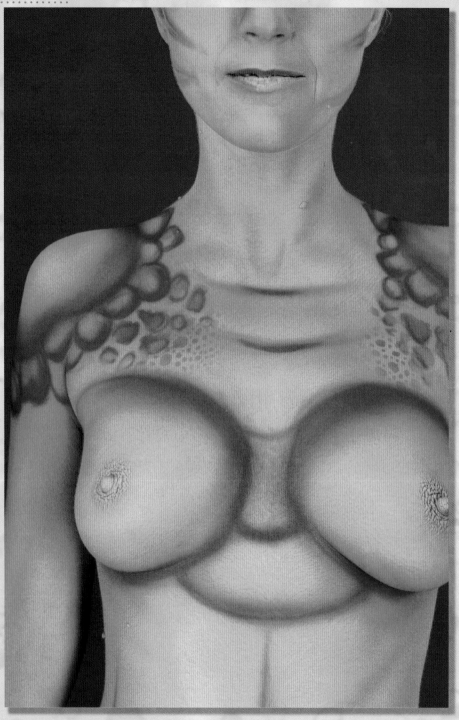

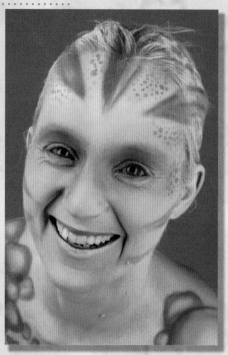

Weiter geht es im Gesicht. Mit der zuletzt verwendeten Schablone werden die kleinen Strukturen jetzt auch in Höhe der Schläfen eingesprüht. Je intensiver Sie das Dunkelgrün über die Schablone sprühen, desto heller oder dunkler werden die Flecken. Größere Muster können Sie auch auf den Haaren verteilen.

Now let´s get on with the face. With the stencil you used last, spray small structures also into the height of the temples. The more intensive you spray the green paint over the stencil, the darker the spots. You can also create some larger patterns on the hair.

Hier sehen Sie die gesamte Strukturierung am Oberkörper. Die mittelgroßen Strukturen wurden freihand teilweise noch mit Dunkelgrün umrandet, um sie optisch den Schulterplatten anzugleichen.

Here you can see the complete structure on the upper body. The middle-sized structures were partially encircled free-hand with dark green to blend them into the shoulder plates.

STEP 14

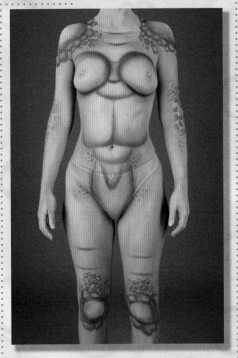

Sprühen Sie mit beiden Schablonen auch Muster am Ellenbogen. Die Knie gestalten Sie genauso wie die Schultern mit einem großen Kreis um die Knie-scheibe und kleiner werdenden Schup-penstrukturen ringsherum.

With these two stencils spray also the pat-terns onto the elbows. Design the knees the same way as the shoulders with a large circle around the kneecap and diminish-ing scaling structures around it.

STEP 15

Zur optischen Verstärkung und mehr Plastizität bekommen die Schuppen im Schulter- und Kniebereich jeweils High-lights. Suchen Sie jeweils die hellsten Stellen der Kreisformen und setzen Sie dort vorsichtig ein wenig Weiß ein.

To provide for a stronger optical effect and more plasticity, highlights will be added to the scaling in the area of the shoulders and of the knees. Find the lightest spot in each of the circle shapes and carefully add a little bit of white.

STEP 16

Hellen Sie bei Bedarf ebenfalls die lich-ten Bereiche der Muskelpartien ein we-nig auf. Auch die Keile auf dem Kopf be-kommen ein Highlight.

If necessary, light up the light areas of the muscle lots. Also the wedges on the head should acquire some highlights.

STEP 17

STEP 18

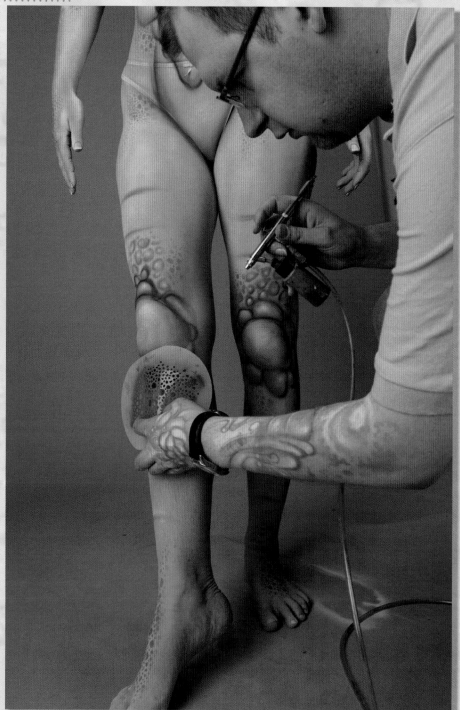

Damit der Kontrast noch ein wenig deutlicher wird, sprühen Sie mit Schwarz die Konturen noch ein wenig nach.

To strengthen the contrast, spray the contours with some black again.

Ist Ihnen die Strukturgebung am Körper noch zu flächig, können Sie wieder mit einer Schablone und dunklem Grün zusätzliche Elemente aufsprühen. Bedenken Sie dabei Hände und Füße. Optional haben Sie auch die Möglichkeit, den Körper mit Sprenklern zu versehen, um ihn noch interessanter wirken zu lassen.

If you think the structure on the body is still too plane for your taste, you can also spray some additional elements with a stencil and dark green. Cover also the hands and the feet with this colour. You now have the option to apply sprinkles onto the body for it to appear even more interesting.

STEP 19

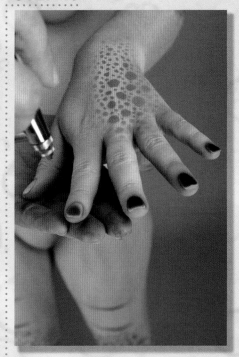

Die Fingernägel werden einfach mit Schwarz eingefärbt.

STEP 20

The finger nails will be simply painted black.

Hier sehen Sie das fertige Alien Girl. Wie eingangs schon erwähnt, können Sie das Motiv auch mit anderen Farben gestalten und mit Hilfe der Schablonen die Strukturierung variieren.

Here you can see the completed Alien Girl. As mentioned above, you can design this motif also with other colours and vary the structures with the help of stencils.

ANGEZOGEN oder auch nicht? Die Imitation von Kleidung ist ein Klassiker des Bodypaintings und hat immer wieder überraschende Wirkungen auf den Betrachter. Den hier gezeigten Badeanzug gibt es nicht von der Stange, denn er entsteht ausschließlich mit Hilfe von klebenden Maskierungen, losen Schablonen und natürlich Bodypainting-Farbe.

DRESSED UP or not? The imitation of clothing is a classic in body painting and again and again surprisingly impresses the viewer. The bathing suit shown here cannot be purchased off the peg because it is an exclusive result of self-adhering friskets, loose stencils and of course body painting paints.

VERWENDETE MATERIALIEN

- Airbrush-Double-Action-Saugsystem
- Bodypainting-Farben: Weiß, Schwarz, Hellgrün, Dunkelgrün, Gelb, Rot, Orange, Blau
- Eigene Schablonen aus Pappe für Blätter, Gürtel und Tukan
- Pinsel

MATERIALS

- *Airbrush double-action bottom-feed system*
- *Body painting paints: white, black, light green, dark green, yellow, red, orange, blue*
- *Self-made stencils cut out of cardboard for the leaves, the belt and the toucan*
- *Paintbrush*

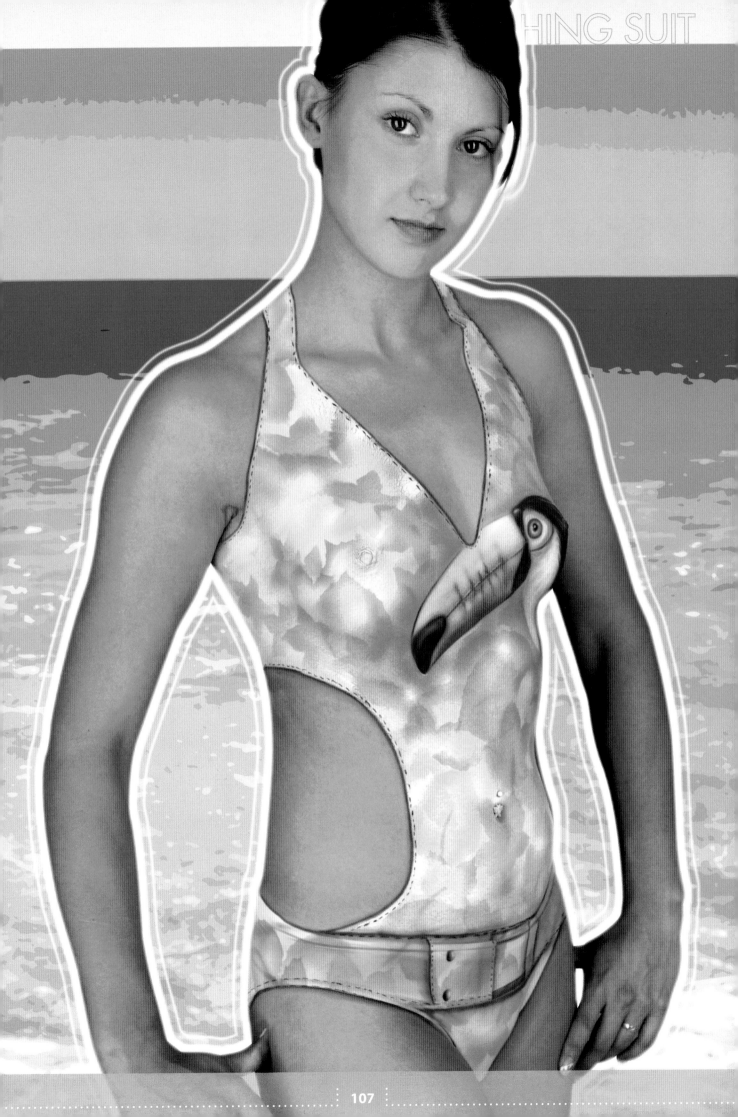

STEP 01

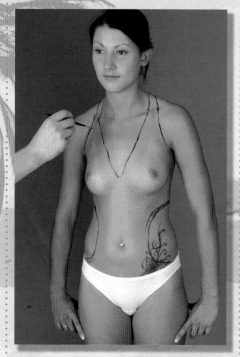

Bevor die weiße Grundierung aufgesprüht wird, werden mit dem Pinsel die Konturen vorgemalt. Ich habe dafür schwarze Farbe benutzt, was sich später allerdings als etwas hinderlich herausgestellt hat. Da die Grundierung Weiß wird, ist es also auch recht hilfreich die Konturen mit Weiß vorzumalen. Evtl. Korrekturen können Sie leicht mit Wasser und Tuch machen.

Before you apply the white basecoat, draw the contours with a paintbrush. I used black colour for this which proved to be somewhat hindering at the end. Because the basecoat will be white, it is also very helpful to pre-draw the contours with white. Potential adjustments can be simply worked out with water and a cloth

STEP 02

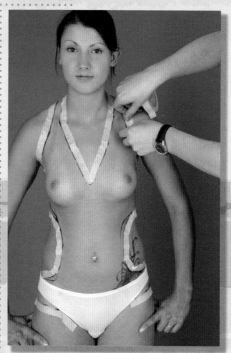

Mit einem klebenden Kreppband werden jetzt die Ränder des Badeanzugs abgeklebt. Dies sorgt für eine scharfe Abgrenzung des Badeanzugs. Das Kreppband lässt sich ganz gut an den Körperrundungen befestigen und macht die Gestaltung erheblich einfacher.

Mask the edges of the bathing suit with a crepe tape. This ensures that you will obtain a sharp-edged border for the bathing suit. The crepe tape is easy to fixate on the body curves and makes the painting a great deal easier.

STEP 03

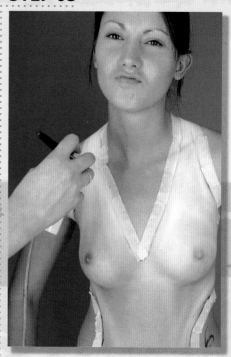

Der maskierte Teil wird nun mit Weiß komplett gleichmäßig ausgesprüht. Overspray können Sie ggf. später mit einem Tuch entfernen.

Spray the masked part completely and evenly with white. You can later remove potential overspray with a cloth.

BADEANZUG

STEP 04

Mit Hilfe einer selbstgeschnittenen Tukan-Schablone wird das Motiv jetzt vorskizziert. Dazu legen Sie einfach das Schabloneninnenteil auf und sprühen mit Gelb an den Konturen entlang.

With the help of a self-made toucan stencil, you can now sketch the motif. To do this, simply place the inner part of the stencil into position and spray with yellow along its contours.

STEP 05

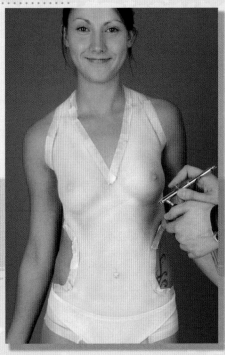

Die Tukan-Fläche müssen Sie jetzt erstmal aussparen. Den Rest des Badeanzugs grundieren Sie fleckig mit Gelb. Dies gibt dem Badeanzug eine Grundfarbe und bildet die Grundlage für den späteren Blätter- und Pflanzen-Hintergrund. Achten Sie auf die abgeklebten Ränder, damit nicht zu viel Overspray auf den Körper gelangt.

The area of the toucan must be spared for now though. Apply a yellow spotted basecoat onto the rest of the bathing suit. This will provide a base colour for the bathing suit and creates a fundament for the later background with leaves and plants. Respect the masked edges to avoid all too much overspray on the body.

STEP 06

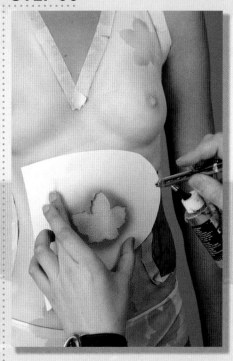

Einige echte Blätter dienten als Vorlage, um aus einem Bogen Papier Schablonen für unterschiedlich große und geformte Pflanzenblätter zu erstellen. Mit dem äußeren Schablonenteil wird das Blattmuster mit unterschiedlichen Farben aufgesprüht. Beginnen Sie mit der größten Blattschablone und sprühen Sie die Form mit einem hellen Grün mehrfach aus.

Several real leaves delivered a template for the creation of plant leaves stencils of various size and shapes out of a paper sheet. The outward part of the stencil can now be sprayed with various colours. Begin with the largest stencil and spray the shape with light green several times.

STEP 07

Arbeiten Sie jetzt mit den kleineren Schablonen weiter. Drehen Sie die Schablone immer wieder ein wenig, um eine unregelmäßige, aber kreative Mischung zu bekommen. Die Blätter sollen sich überlagern, so dass ein Geflecht aus Blattmustern entsteht.

Work on with the smaller stencils now. Rotate the stencil every time a bit to obtain an uneven but creative mix. The leaves should interfere with each other so to create a netting of leaf patterns.

STEP 08

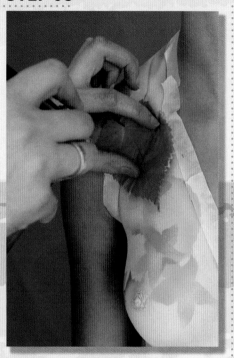

Sprühen Sie auch mit einem dunkleren Grün weitere Blattmuster auf. Durch den Abstand zum Körper können Sie die Deckkraft der Farben steuern und unterschiedliche Nuancen und transparente Effekte erzielen.
Nutzen Sie dafür auch Originalblätter und sprühen Sie an der Außenkante entlang, um die Kantenstruktur abzubilden.

Spray other leaf pattern with dark green. You can control the opacity of the colours through the distance to the body and so obtain various nuances and transparent effects.
Use for this the same real leaves and spray along the outer edge to imitate the edge structure.

STEP 09

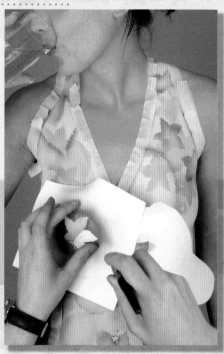

Damit die Tukan-Form weiterhin weiß bleibt, können Sie die innere Tukan-Schablone zur Abdeckung benutzen und darüber die Blatt-Schablone positionieren.

To keep the toucan shape white, you can use the inner stencil of the toucan stencil for masking and position the leaf stencil over it.

STEP 10

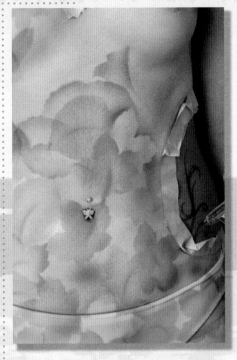

Mit dunklem Grün können Sie ein paar Striche als Äste bzw. Blattadern innerhalb der Blätter sprühen. Wenn Sie das Blattmuster noch ein wenig harmonischer zu einer Einheit verbinden möchten, können Sie z.B. mit Gelb partiell noch die eine oder andere Stelle einnebeln.

Use dark green to spray some lines to create branches or respectively leaf veins in the leaves. If you want to band the leaves pattern into a more harmonizing unit, you can for example partially spray the one or the other spot with yellow.

STEP 11

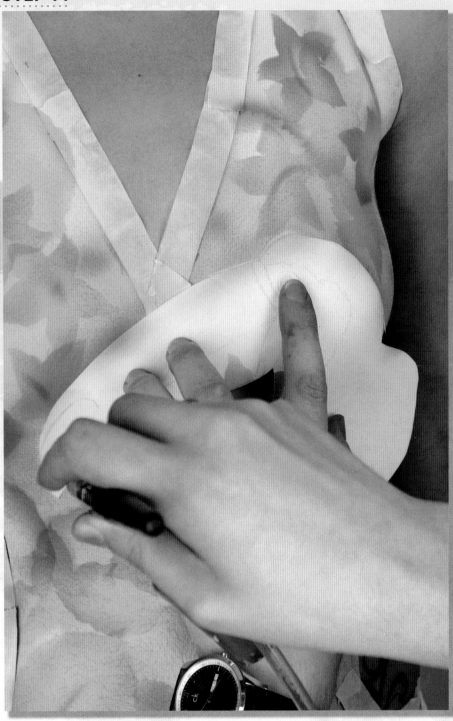

Positionieren Sie nun nochmal die innere Tukan-Schablone und nebeln Sie dunkles Grün über den Badeanzug, damit später der Kontrast zum Tukan noch ein wenig deutlicher wird.

Position now the inner toucan stencil again and overspray the bathing suit with dark green to obtain a sharper contrast to the toucan later.

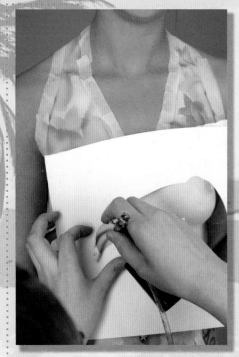  

Jetzt geht es mit der äußeren Tukan-Schablone weiter. Legen Sie diese wieder direkt auf die Position und sprühen Sie als erstes mit Schwarz die Schnabel-Spitze aus. Diese wird im vorderen Bereich durch die Schablone geformt, den Rest formen Sie freihand. Sprühen Sie dabei wieder vorsichtig mit einem geringen Abstand zum Modell, damit dieser Bereich eine scharfe Kontur bekommt. Orientieren Sie sich am besten an einem Foto eines Tukans, damit Sie wissen, wo Sie welche Farbtöne einsetzen müssen.

Ebenfalls mit Schwarz arbeiten Sie noch den Übergang vom Schnabel zum Kopf sowie das schwarze Gefieder aus. Während Sie das Gefieder brushen, können Sie auch die Außenschablone schon beiseite legen und freihand arbeiten, da das Gefieder keine extrem scharfe Kante benötigt. Brushen Sie ein linienartiges Geflecht, um dem Gefieder Struktur zu geben.

Positionieren Sie danach wieder die Schablone und sprühen Sie den Schnabel flächig mit Gelb aus. Achten Sie darauf, dass die schwarzen Schnabelbereiche dabei nicht so viel Overspray abbekommen.

Now we get on with the outer toucan stencil. Place it again into position and spray first of all the tip of the beak with black. This tip will be shaped by the stencil in the front part and free-hand in the rest. Again, spray carefully from a small distance to the model´s body to obtain a sharp contour in this area. It is the best to get a good idea of a toucan´s look with the help of a photo so that you know where and which colour tones you need to apply.

You will also use black to work out the gradation from the beak to the head as well as the feathers. While brushing the feathers, you can put the outer stencil aside and work free-hand as there is no need for sharp edges in the feathers. Brush a line-like netting to give the feathers some structure.

Position the stencil again and spray the whole area of the beak with yellow. Remember that better less than a lot of overspray should get onto the black areas of the beak.

STEP 15

Sprühen Sie mit Rot die mittlere Schnabellinie ein. Auch hier ist ein geringer Abstand zum Modell nötig, um eine intensive Linie zu erhalten.

Spray the middle beak line with red. Here also, a small distance to the model´s body is necessary to obtain an intensive line.

STEP 16

Ebenfalls mit Rot bekommt der Schnabel im unteren Bereich einen orangefarbenen Verlauf. Das Gerät wird dafür ein wenig weiter vom Malgrund entfernt. Obwohl Sie mit Rot sprühen, können Sie durch die Farbüberlagerung auf dem gelben Schnabeluntergrund einen Orange-Farbton erzielen.

Using red, the beak obtains an orange-coloured gradation in its lower area. For this, hold the device in a bigger distance to the working surface. Even though you spray with red, you can obtain an orange colour tone through the interference of the overlaying colour on the yellow background of the beak

STEP 17

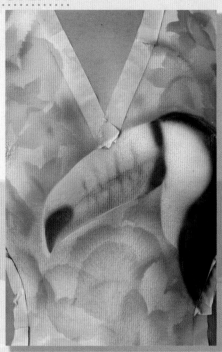

Sprühen Sie nun mit leicht gezitterten Linien und roter Farbe die typischen senkrechten Strukturen des Schnabels ein.

Now spray slightly shaky, red lines to create the typical upright structures of the beak.

STEP 18

STEP 19

STEP 20

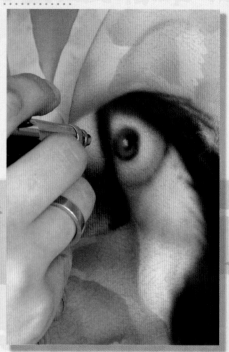

Weiter geht es mit dem Auge. Sprühen Sie eine weiche Kreisform aus Gelb und Rot/Orange um das spätere Auge herum. Lassen Sie dabei den mittleren Augenbereich noch frei, danach füllen Sie diesen mit Blau aus.

Greifen Sie jetzt wieder zu der schwarzen Farbe. Sprühen Sie um den blauen Augenbereich vorsichtig eine schwarze Schattierung. Außerdem definieren Sie mit Schwarz die Iris des Auges und den Übergang vom Augenbereich zum Gefieder. Wenn Sie das Gerät mit ein wenig Entfernung vom Körper halten und nur wenig den Hebel nach hinten ziehen, können Sie den Schatten unter dem Schnabel sprühen. Bei Bedarf können Sie auch noch das Gefieder optimieren. Einige Übergänge werden mit dünnen Strichen aus dem Gefieder heraus in den Hintergrund oder ins helle Gefieder gezogen.

Die Reflexion im Auge sprühen Sie vorsichtig mit Weiß ein. Gehen Sie dabei dicht an den Körper und drücken Sie erstmal nur den Hebel runter. Dann ziehen Sie den Hebel vorsichtig nach hinten, damit nur ganz wenig Farbe austritt. Alternativ können Sie für die Reflexion auch einen Pinsel benutzen.

Let´s get on with the eye. Spray a soft circle shape with yellow and red/orange around the later eye. While spraying, spare the middle of the eye area to subsequently fill it with blue.

Grab again the black paint. Spray carefully a black shading around the blue area in the eye. Also, define the iris of the eye and the transition of the eye to the feathers with black. When you hold the device in a small distance to the body and pull the trigger back only slightly, you can spray the shading underneath the beak. You can also optimize the feathers if necessary. Some transitions will be developed in thin lines out of the feathers toward the background or toward the lighter feathers.

Spray the reflection in the eye carefully with white. Approach the body closely for this and for starters, only press the trigger. Then carefully pull it back so that only a tiny amount of paint comes out. For this reflection, you can also use a paintbrush.

BADEANZUG

STEP 21

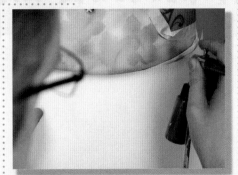

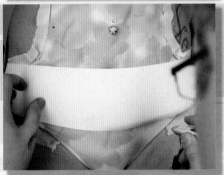

Um den Kleidungseindruck noch zu verfeinern, soll der Badeanzug zusätzlich einen Gürtel bekommen. Schneiden Sie hierfür zwei weitere lose Schablone zurecht. Da ein ganz gerades Stück Pappe nicht der Gürtelform entspricht, schneiden Sie die Schablonen etwas bogenförmig aus. Sprühen Sie dann mit Dunkelgrün an den Kanten entlang, um den Schatten des Gürtels zu simulieren.

To improve the impression of the clothing, the bathing suit should in addition obtain a belt. For this purpose, cut out two other loose stencils. Because an entirely straight piece of cardboard doesn´t correspond with the form of a belt, cut the stencil somewhat curved. Spray then along the edges with dark green to simulate the shadow of the belt.

STEP 22

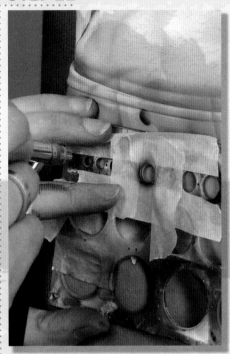

Mit einer geraden Papierkante formen Sie die Laschen und Ösen des Gürtels. Für die Nieten verwenden Sie eine Kreisschablone. Sprühen Sie die linke Seite des Kreises mit Schwarz an und die rechte Seite mit Weiß.

You can now form the clips and the thread eyes of the belt. Use a circle stencil for the blanks. Spray the left side of the circle with black and the right side with white.

STEP 23

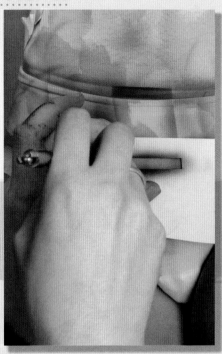

Mit einer kleinen rechteckigen Schablone sprühen Sie zwei horizontale Balken für die Gürtelschnalle. Sprühen Sie dann auch die Gürtel- und Laschenkanten noch einmal leicht mit Schwarz an, um den Schatten zu verstärken.

Using a small rectangular stencil, spray two horizontal bars for the belt buckle. Then, spray the edges of the belt and the clips with black again to strengthen the shading.

STEP 24

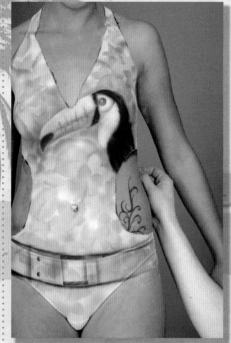

Es wird Zeit, die Kreppbandmaskierung des Badeanzugs abzunehmen. Nun sehen Sie zum ersten Mal den kompletten Badeanzug.

It is time to remove the crepe tape masking of the bathing suit. For the first time, you can see the complete bathing suit.

STEP 25

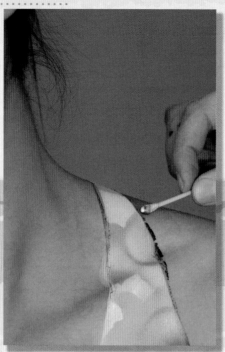

Wenn Sie einige kleinere Bereiche mit Fehlern oder Overspray korrigieren möchten, können Sie ein mit Wasser getränktes Wattestäbchen oder ein Papiertuch verwenden.

When you want to adjust some smaller inaccuracies or overspray, you can use a cotton bud soaked with water, or a paper towel.

STEP 26

Zum Abschluss soll der Badeanzug noch eine Naht erhalten. Benutzen Sie dafür Schwarz und eine kleine Pinselgröße. Malen Sie kleine Striche am Rand entlang. Auch der Gürtel erhält Nähte. Hierbei ist es zu empfehlen, entsprechendes Fotomaterial zu studieren.

Finally, the bathing suit should obtain a seam. For this, use black colour and a small-sized paintbrush. Paint small dashes along the edge. The belt as well will obtain seams. It is recommended to study appropriate photo samples.

STEP 27

Damit sich der Badeanzug noch ein wenig mehr vom Körper abhebt, können Sie vorsichtig mit Schwarz am Rand eine leichte Schattierung sprühen. Der Schatten sollte dabei nicht zu breit werden, da der Badeanzug ja eng anliegt. Sprühen Sie deshalb nur mit einem geringen Abstand zum Modell.

To silhouette the bathing suite a bit more and visually lift it off the body, you can carefully spray a light black shadow on its edges. The shadow should not be too wide as the bathing suit fits the body very closely. Thus, you will spray only from a tiny distance from the model´s body.

STEP 28

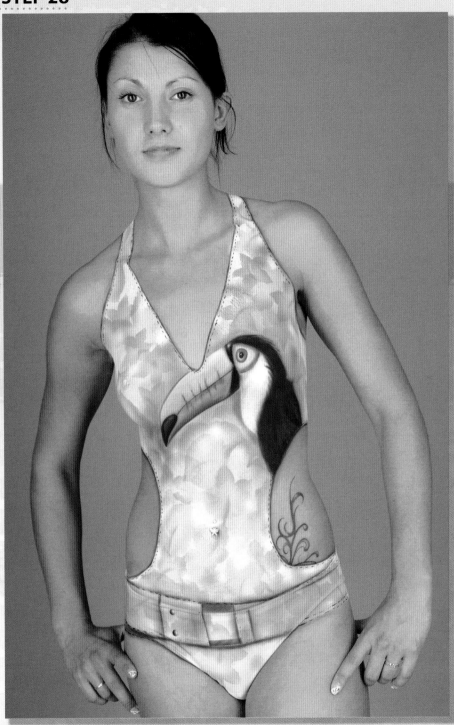

Hier sehen Sie das fertige Schwimm-Outfit!

Here you can see the finished swimming outfit!

ROBOTER UND KÜNSTLICHE MENSCHEN faszinieren die Wissenschaft schon seit über 100 Jahren. Doch die perfekte Imitation des Menschen ist bislang noch nicht gelungen. Ganz im Gegensatz zur Imitation des Roboters: Als Bodypainting lässt sich der menschliche Körper ganz einfach in eine Maschine aus glänzendem Chrom verwandeln. Der Fantasie sind dabei keine Grenzen gesetzt. Das Motiv erfordert allerdings schon einen recht sicheren Umgang mit dem Airbrushgerät, denn es wird fast vollständig freihand gestaltet. Erst der gezielte Einsatz von Reflexionen, Lichtern und Farbverläufen lässt den realistischen Chromeffekt entstehen.

THE SCHOLARS HAVE BEEN FASCINATED by the robots and androids for more than 100 years. However, nobody has yet succeeded in matters of a perfect imitation of the human being, quite opposite to a perfect imitation of a robot: As for body painting, the human body can be transformed into a machine made out of shiny chrome very simply. The limits of your imagination are the limits of what is possible. The motif certainly requires some well mastered handling of the airbrush device because it is to be created almost completely free-hand. The realistic chrome effect will emerge only thanks to the well-directed application of reflections, lights and colour gradients.

VERWENDETE MATERIALIEN

- ▶ Airbrush-Double-Action-Saugsystem
- ▶ Airbrush-Double-Action-Fließsystem
- ▶ Bodypainting-Farben: Weiß, Schwarz, Blau, Beige
- ▶ Kreisschablone

MATERIALS

- ▶ *Airbrush double-action bottom-feed system*
- ▶ *Airbrush double-action gravity-feed system*
- ▶ *Body painting paints: white, black, blue, beige*
- ▶ *Circle stencil*

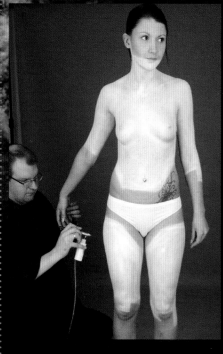
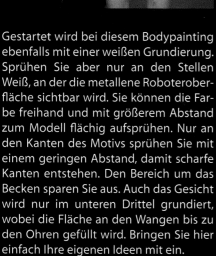

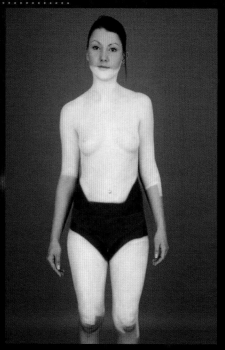

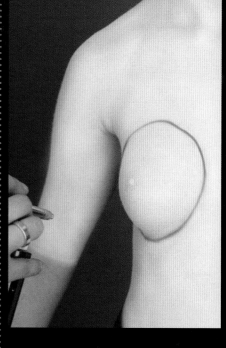

Gestartet wird bei diesem Bodypainting ebenfalls mit einer weißen Grundierung. Sprühen Sie aber nur an den Stellen Weiß, an der die metallene Roboteroberfläche sichtbar wird. Sie können die Farbe freihand und mit größerem Abstand zum Modell flächig aufsprühen. Nur an den Kanten des Motivs sprühen Sie mit einem geringen Abstand, damit scharfe Kanten entstehen. Den Bereich um das Becken sparen Sie aus. Auch das Gesicht wird nur im unteren Drittel grundiert, wobei die Fläche an den Wangen bis zu den Ohren gefüllt wird. Bringen Sie hier einfach Ihre eigenen Ideen mit ein.

Im Bereich des Beckens wird die ausgesparte Fläche Schwarz grundiert. An dieser Stelle werden später Kabel und Lichter angedeutet.

Mit Schwarz werden auch die Segmente der Roboterrüstung eingezeichnet. Dies wird freihand gemacht und erfordert hohe Konzentration. Damit die Linien einigermaßen gerade werden, sollte das Modell recht still stehen. Sprühen Sie kreisrunde Linien um die Brüste herum.

To get started with this body painting, apply a white basecoat in the first step. However, only spray the white on the spots where the metallic surface of the robot will be visible. You can continuously spray the paint free-hand and from a bigger distance to the model´s skin. Only at the edges of the motif you should spray from a smaller distance to create harder edges. Spare the area around the pelvis. Apply the white basecoat only onto the lowest third of the face so that the area between the cheeks and the ears is fully covered. Simply put your own ideas into work here.

Now create a black basecoat in the area of the pelvis which you spared before. On this spot, you will later create some cords and lights.

Also with black, paint the segments of the robot´s armature. Do this freehand and focus tightly. The model should stand still so that you can create reasonably straight lines. Spray circular lines around the breasts.

STEP 04

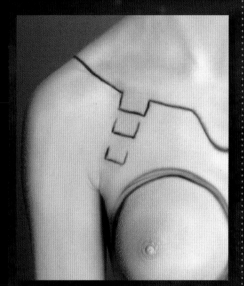

Weiter geht es mit den Linien auf dem Brustbein. Um den technischen Aspekt zu verdeutlichen, werden runde Ausbuchten sowie eckige Formen und Unterbrechungen aufgetragen. Das gesamte Motiv soll symmetrisch ausgewogen aufgetragen werden, daher erfordert auch der Auftrag der halbrunden Form am Brustkorb eine ruhige Hand.

Now let´s get on with the lines on the breastbone. To underscore the technical aspects, create round recesses as well as square shapes and gaps. The complete motif should be created in a symmetrical, balanced way, and so the application of the half-round shape on the chest requires a calm hand.

STEP 05

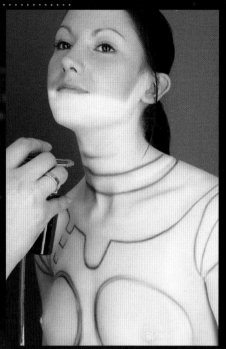

An den Gelenken bekommt unser Modell „bewegliche Glieder". Im Bild sehen Sie, wie die Segmente am Hals aufgesprüht werden.

Create the appearance of flexible limbs at the joints of the model. The picture shows the segments being sprayed on the neck.

STEP 06

Auch an den Schultergelenken und an den Armbeugen sprühen Sie die beweglichen Gliederbereiche auf. Zusätzliche Linien und Detailelemente am Bauch, an der Brust, im Gesicht und an den Armen und Beinen verdeutlichen den technischen Charakter des Motivs. Arbeiten Sie dabei mit einem geringen Abstand zum Körper, damit die Linien scharf und deutlich erkennbar sind. Da hier eher wenig Farbe zur Verwendung kommt, kann an dieser Stelle auch mit einem Fließsystem gearbeitet werden.

Spray the areas of the flexible limbs also on the shoulder and elbow joints. Additional lines and detailed elements on the belly, on the chest, in the face as well as on the arms and legs will further underscore the technical character of the motif. Work from a close distance to the body so that the lines are sharp and distinct. Since the amount of used paint is small on these spots, you can also work with a gravity-feed system.

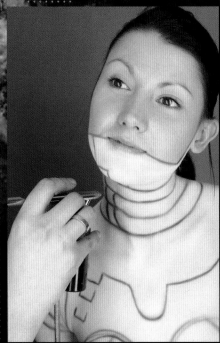

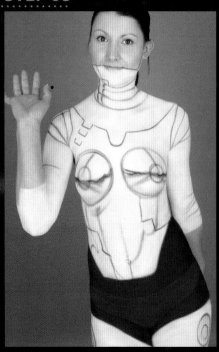

Damit die Roboterstruktur metallisch wirkt, bekommt das Modell einen Chromlook. Da Chrom keine Farbe ist, die man kaufen und aufsprühen kann, simulieren Sie die Chromoptik mit Hilfe von Spiegelungen aus scharfen dunklen Kanten und kombinierten Farbverläufen. Mit Schwarz sprühen Sie dafür zunächst einmal die dunklen Reflexionen auf. Bei den Halsglieder-Elementen sind das jeweils zwei schwarze vertikale und kurvige Striche.

Die Brustplatten bekommen ebenfalls eine Reflexion eingesprüht. Eine leicht gezitterte Linienstruktur simuliert später eine landschaftliche Spiegelung auf der Oberfläche. Sprühen Sie auch einen leichten Verlauf unterhalb der Linienstruktur auf. Zusätzliche Reflexionslinien erzeugen Sie an den Armgelenken und Schulterelementen. Im Bild sehen Sie auch ein paar grobe Andeutungen für Farbverläufe im Bauchbereich.

Nehmen Sie jetzt die blaue Farbe und sprühen Sie Schattierungen an den Halsgelenken, ausgehend von den schwarzen Bogenlinien sowie im oberen Bereich der Brustplatten. Achten Sie darauf, dass noch weiße Lichtbereiche innerhalb der Hals- und Brustelemente stehen bleiben.

To make the robot structure appear metallic, the model will be given a chrome look. Because chrome is no colour you could just buy and spray, simulate the chrome appearance with the help of reflections created with dark hard edges and combined colour gradients. First of all, spray the dark reflections with black. As for the neck joints, two black vertical and curved lines each are necessary.

Also the sheets on the chest will obtain a sprayed-on reflection. A slightly shaky line structure will later simulate a scenic reflection on the surface. Spray a light gradient also underneath this line structure. Create some additional reflection lines on the arm joints and shoulder elements. On the picture you can also see some rough indications of colour gradients in the belly area.

Now grab the blue paint and spray the shadings on the neck joints starting at the black curved lines as well as those in the upper area of the chest sheets. Make sure that you still spare some white light area within the neck and chest elements.

SEXY ROBOT

STEP 10

STEP 11

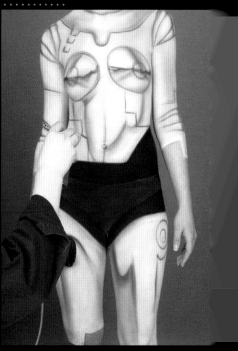

Arbeiten Sie so den ganzen Körper mi den blauen Reflexionen aus, also auch am Bauch und an den Oberschenkeln

Proceeding as shown above, work out the blue reflections on the whole body including the belly and the thighs.

Sprühen Sie das Blau auch im Gesicht und am Brustkorb, an den Schultergelenken und an den Brustplatten. Die Farbverläufe sind jeweils immer von den schwarzen Lini-en ausgehend aufzutragen. Arbeiten Sie im Bereich der schwarzen Linien noch recht dicht am Modell, damit das Blau dort intensiver wirkt, und erhöhen Sie den Abstand, damit die Farbe in den weißen Bereich ausläuft.

Spray blue also in the face and on the chest, shoulder joints and chest sheets. The colour gradients are to be applied starting always at the black lines. In the area close to the black lines, work still from a close distance to the model to allow a more intensive blue to emerge, and increase the working distance to make the colour fade out in the white areas.

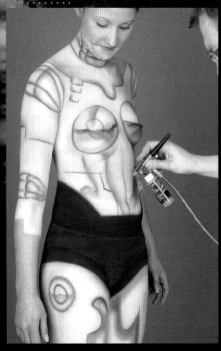

Die Chromreflexion spiegelt eine sandige Dünenlandschaft wieder, daher tragen Sie mit Beige zusätzliche Farbverläufe auf. Sprühen Sie von dem blauen Farbverlauf beginnend in den weißen Farbbereich hinein.

The chrome reflection mirrors a sandy dune scenery and therefore, you apply some more colour gradients with beige. Begin spraying at the blue colour gradient and let the colour fade out into the white.

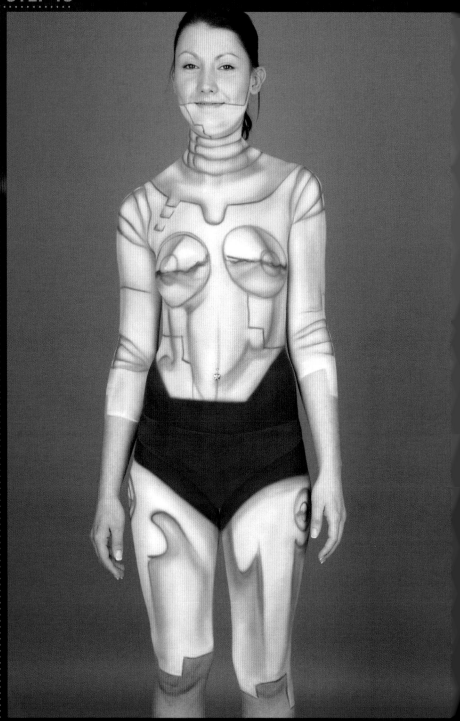

Hier sehen Sie den Zwischenstand. Treten Sie zurück und begutachten Sie den bisherigen Farbauftrag. Vergleichen Sie ihn auch mit Ihrer Skizze. Einige Bereiche müssen in den nächsten Schritten noch optimiert und verfeinert werden.

Here you can see the preliminary result. Step back and render an opinion to the paint application. Check it against your sketch. You will have to optimize and refine some areas in the next steps.

STEP 14

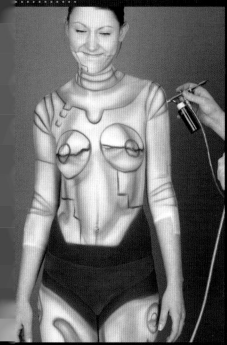

STEP 15

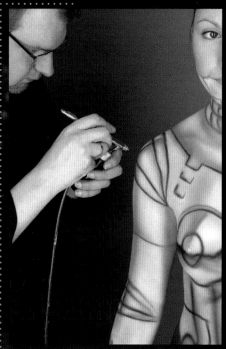

STEP 16

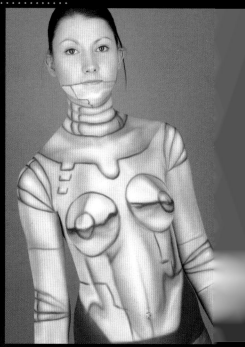

Mit Blau werden einige Bereiche noch-mal überarbeitet und intensiviert. Auch die weißen Bereiche der Roboter-Rüs-tung bekommen blaue Schattierungen wie zum Beispiel am Arm, Bauch oder Brustkorb. Durch die zusätzlichen Farb-aufträge werden die schwarzen Linien ggf. ein wenig überdeckt, daher ist es ratsam, diese nochmal mit Schwarz zu überarbeiten.

Um die schwarzen Linien und Details ge-nau zu platzieren, ist es hilfreich, wenn Sie die andere Hand zur Unterstützung der Geräteführung benutzen.

Mit Weiß werden in diesem Schritt ei-nige Highlights eingearbeitet, so das die Gelenkelemente dreidimensionale erscheinen und die Chromteile meh Glanz erhalten. Das Motiv bekomm dadurch zusätzlich mehr Kontrast und Frische.

Rework and intensify some areas with blue. Also the white areas of the robot´s armature should obtain blue shadings; so for example the arms, belly or the chest. Due to the additional paint application, the black lines might have become some-what covered, and it will be better to re-work them with black.

To place the black lines and details accu-rately, it is helpful to use the other hand for better device control.

In this step, you integrate some highlight. so that the joint elements appear three-dimensional and the chrome parts shine up even more. This way, the motif obtain additional contrast and freshness.

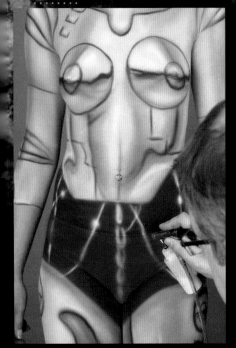

Jetzt ist der schwarze Bereich zwischen dem oberen und unteren Rüstungsteil dran. Sprühen Sie mit Weiß einige verbindende Linien von oben nach unten. Diese sollen Kabel und Verstrebungen darstellen, die die Teile miteinander verbinden. Mit Sprühpunkten setzen Sie Lichter auf diese Kabelstränge. Das Motiv wirkt jetzt, also ob Ober- und Unterteil der Rüstung getrennt voneinander „schweben".

Now it is time to work on the black area between the upper and lower parts of the armature. From the top down, spray several connecting lines with white. These should constitute cords and cross beams bonding the parts. Spraying some spray dots, you put some lights onto the wiring harnesses. The upper and the lower part of the motif's armature now appear to be somehow "floating", independent from each other.

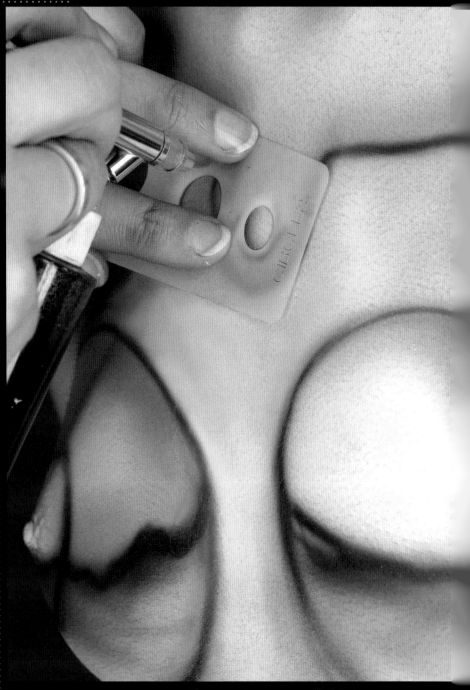

Zum Schluss werden am Roboter-Outfit noch Nieten hinzugefügt. Diese passen seh gut zum Gesamtkonzept und bieten dem Betrachter zusätzliche Blickpunkte. Bevo Sie mit der Schablone die Niete scharfkantig aufsprühen, brushen Sie als erstes mi Schwarz freihand die dunklen Schattierung im Halbkreis auf. Mit Weiß sprühen Sie di andere Hälfte des Halbkreises. Auf diese Licht- und Schattenandeutung wird dann di Niete gesetzt. Suchen Sie sich eine passende Kreisschablone aus oder schneiden Sie mit dem Kreisschneider eine Lochgröße aus.

Finally, add some rivets to the robot's outfit. They match the overall concept very well and offer additional potential for the observer's eye. Before you spray the hard-edged rivet: using a stencil, brush the half-circled, dark shading free-hand with black. Spray the other half of the circle with white. Then, create the rivets on these indications of light and shade

STEP 19

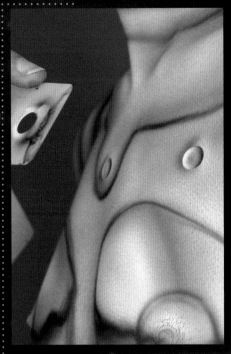

STEP 20

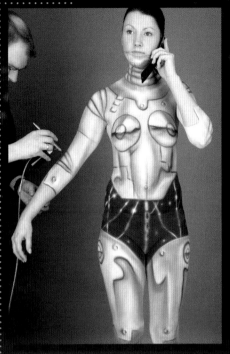

STEP 21

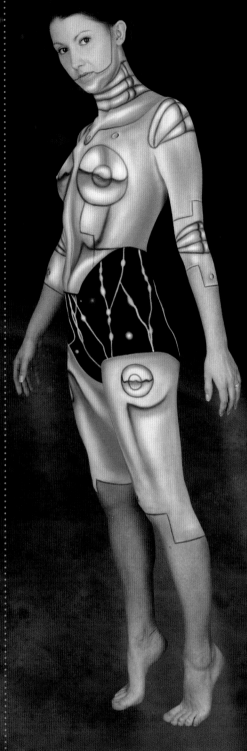

Sprühen Sie dann innerhalb der Kreisschablone rechts mit Schwarz und links mit Weiß. Da Sie sicherlich mehrere Nieten am Körper aufsprühen, ist es ratsam erst immer mit einer Farbe (in diesem Fall Schwarz) alle Schatten und Füllungen zu sprühen und später dann erneut mit der Schablone anzusetzen und mit Weiß zu arbeiten.

Zusätzliche Nieten können Sie an den Armen und an den Oberschenkeln einbauen. Überprüfen Sie bei diesen letzten Arbeitsschritten nochmal alle Details, Kontraste und Farben und führen Sie ggf. Korrekturen durch.

Then, spray black onto the right within the circle stencil and white onto the left. As you certainly will spray several rivets onto the body, you are well advised to always spray all the shades and fillings first with one colour (in this case black), and later place the stencil again onto the right spot and work with white.

You can also create some additional rivets on the arms and thighs. As you carry out these last work steps, check again all the details, contrasts and colours, and if necessary, apply corrections.

Das fertige Motiv – Ihr Roboter ist nun bereit fürs Fotoshooting.

The completed motif – your robot is now ready for the photo shooting.

CORSAGE

MIT EINFACHSTEN HILFSMITTELN lassen sich beim Airbrush-Bodypainting überraschende Effekte erstellen. Ein Beispiel dafür ist diese Mieder-Corsage. Das Wäschestück sieht täuschend echt aus: Erreicht wurde dieser Look durch ein altes Stück Gardine. Lassen Sie sich verführen…

IN BODY PAINTING, IT IS POSSIBLE to create surprising effects with the simplest means. The following corsage is a good example. This piece of clothing looks deceivingly real: this look was obtained with the help of an old piece of curtain drapery. Let us seduce you...

VERWENDETE MATERIALIEN
- ▶ Airbrush-Saugsystem, Airbrush-Fließsystem
- ▶ Bodypainting-Farben: Weiß, Beige (Hautfarbe), Grau
- ▶ Pinsel, Gardinen-Stoff
- ▶ Papier, Cutter

MATERIALS
- ▶ *Airbrush bottom-feed system, Airbrush gravity-feed system*
- ▶ *Body painting paints: white, beige (skin tone), grey*
- ▶ *Paintbrush, curtain drapery*
- ▶ *Paper, cutter*

STEP 01

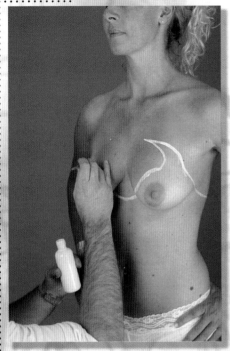

Mit einem Pinsel und Weiß malen Sie die Kontur der Mieder-Corsage auf. In dieser Phase der Entstehung können Sie noch jederzeit die Konturen ändern, falls die Form z.B. nicht symmetrisch läuft. Mit Wasser können Sie die Farbe einfach entfernen.

First, draw the white contours of the corsage with a paintbrush. At this stage of work, you can still alter the contours anytime, for example when the shapes are not symmetrical. You can simply remove the paint with water.

STEP 02

Die gesamte Konturzeichnung wird nun mit Weiß gleichmäßig ausgesprüht. Wenn Sie genau arbeiten, können Sie das komplett freihand bzw. mit Hilfe einer losen Schablone machen. Schneiden Sie mit einem Cutter aus einem großen Bogen Papier eine kurvige Schablone aus. Diese kann dann flexibel an den Konturen angelegt werden, um den nichtbemalten Körperbereich zu schützen und eine scharfe Kante zu erhalten.

Spray the whole of the contour draft evenly with white. When you work precisely, you can do this completely free-hand or respectively with the help of loose stencils. Cut a curved stencil out of a large sheet of paper with a cutter. This stencil can then be flexibly positioned at the contours to protect the body areas which should not be painted and to obtain sharp edges.

STEP 03

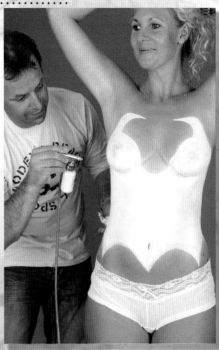

Achten Sie darauf, dass der Farbauftrag gleichmäßig wird, damit die Corsage nicht fleckig wirkt.

Remember to apply the paint evenly to avoid stains on the corsage.

STEP 04

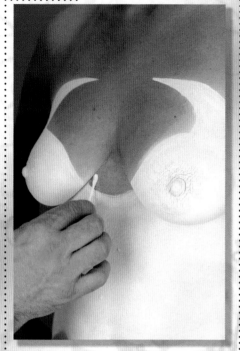

Overspray können Sie gezielt mit einem Wattestäbchen oder einem Tuch und Wasser entfernen.

If necessary, you can remove overspray with a cotton bud or a cloth and water.

STEP 05

Mischen Sie sich nun mit Braun und Weiß sowie ggf. zusätzlich etwas Gelb und Rot einen zum Modell passenden Hautton an. Um das Mieder-Muster zu erzeugen, benutzen Sie ein Stück gemusterte Gardine. Legen Sie sie über den Bauch des Modells. Es ist hilfreich, wenn das Modell die Maskierung festhält.

Now mix brown and white as well as possibly some yellow and red to obtain a colour tone matching the skin tone of the model. To create the pattern of the corsage, use a piece of curtain drapery. Place it onto the belly of the model. It is very helpful when the model holds the masking in its position.

STEP 06

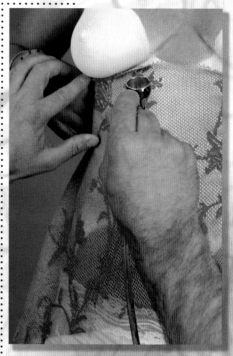

Sprühen Sie nun mit dem Hautton über die Gardine. Dabei ist es wichtig, dass Sie gleich beim ersten Sprühgang ausreichend Kontrast aufbauen. Halten Sie den jeweiligen Teil der Gardine, an dem Sie gerade arbeiten, immer mit der linken Hand fest und drücken Sie ihn vorsichtig an. Nur so kann das Muster nicht verwackeln und die Konturen werden scharf.

Spray the skin-toned paint onto the curtain masking. It is important to create a sufficient contrast already with the first spray layer. Hold the particular part of the curtain, on which you are currently working, with the left hand and press it carefully onto the skin. This is the way to a stable pattern with sharp contours.

STEP 07

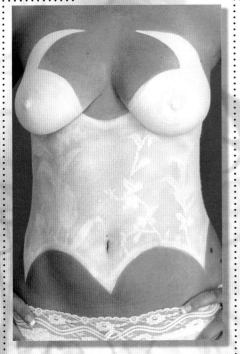

Hier sehen Sie den Zwischenstand. Am Rand des Mieders wurde beim Sprühen ca. ein Zentimeter freigelassen.

Here you can see the preliminary result. At the edge of the corsage, about 1 cm, was spared.

STEP 08

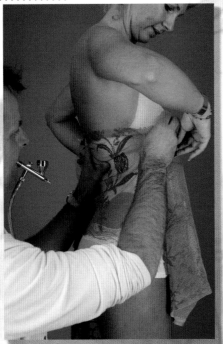

Arbeiten Sie am Rücken des Modells genauso weiter.

Work on the back of the model exactly the same way.

STEP 09

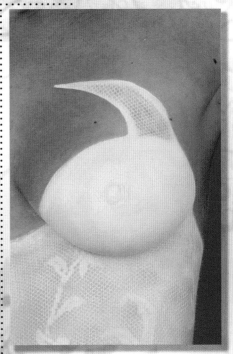

Auch oberhalb der Brust verwenden Sie das Gardinenmuster. Arbeiten Sie dicht am Modell, damit zum „BH-Körbchen" hin eine scharfe Kontur entsteht, denn das Körbchen soll kein Spitzenmuster erhalten.

Use the curtain pattern also above the chest. Work in a very close distance to the working surface so that you create a sharp contour toward the "bra cup" because the cups will not be be given the lace pattern.

STEP 10

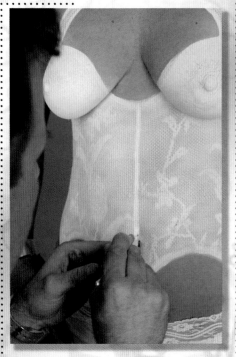

Mit Weiß korrigieren und verstärken Sie die Ränder der Corsage. Außerdem sprühen Sie vertikal über den Bauch eine schmale weiße Linie. Dies ist eine Strebe der Corsage. Arbeiten Sie dicht am Körper. Alternativ können Sie die Strebe auch mit dem Pinsel ziehen.

Adjust and strengthen the edges of the corsage with white. Also, spray a thin, vertical white line across the belly. This is the stiffener of the corsage. Work very closely to the body. To draw the stiffener, you can alternatively use a paintbrush.

STEP 11

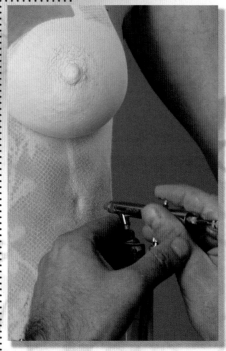

Weitere Streben sprühen Sie unterhalb der Brüste nach unten hin. Wenn Sie die linke Hand zur Stabilisierung benutzen, können Sie die Streben ohne Probleme freihand brushen.

Spray the other stiffeners underneath the breasts with a downward movement. When you use your left hand to gain more stability, you can brush the stiffeners freehand at no effort.

STEP 12

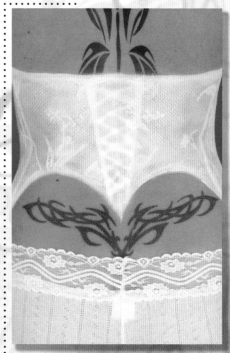

Arbeiten Sie ebenfalls auf dem Rücken Streben ein. Die Schnürung der Corsage wird auch mit Weiß vorgelegt.

Work out the stiffeners also on the back. Outline also the cording of the corsage with white.

CORSAGE

STEP 13

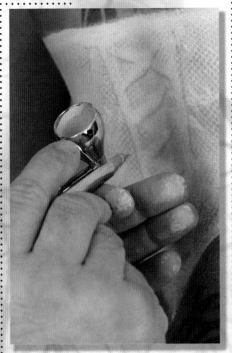

Mit einem helleren Grauton brushen Sie nun feine Konturen an den Verstrebungen und den inneren Rändern des Mieders entlang. Dies gibt eine Schattenwirkung und erhöht den Kontrast.

Now brush some finer contours along the bracing and the inner edges of the corsage with light grey. This will provide for a shadow appearance and also, it will sharpen the contrast.

STEP 14

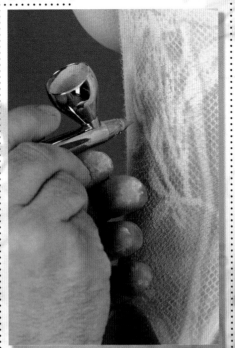

Auch die Schnürung und die floralen Muster erhalten jeweils an der Unterseite eine graue Schattierung, um die Plastizität hervorzuheben. Achten Sie bei der gekreuzten Schnürung darauf, welche Bänder oben und welche unten liegen. Sprühen Sie mit einem geringen Abstand zum Modell, damit eine feine Linienstärke erreicht wird.

The cording and the floral pattern should each obtain a grey shadow on their bottom edge to accentuate the plasticity. As the parts of the cord cross each other, remember to respect which ones lie underneath the others. Spray from a close distance to the model to obtain a fine line width.

STEP 15

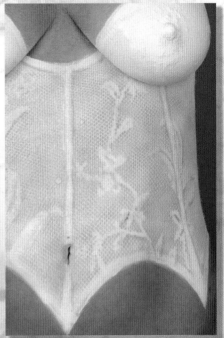

Hier sehen Sie den aktuellen Zwischenstand.

Here you can once again see the preliminary result.

STEP 16

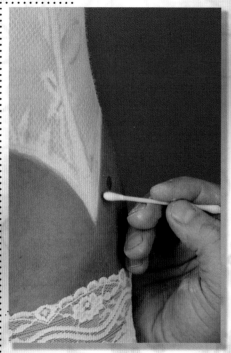

Mit einem Wattestäbchen und Wasser haben Sie jetzt wieder die Gelegenheit, Korrekturen vorzunehmen.

Now you have the opportunity for adjustments using a cotton bud and water, if necessary.

STEP 17

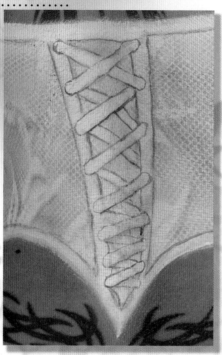

Damit die Schnürung noch ein wenig scharfkantiger und konstrastreicher wirkt, benutzen Sie einen feinen Pinsel für die Details.

Use a fine paintbrush for details so to make the cording even more hard-edged and richer in contrast.

STEP 18

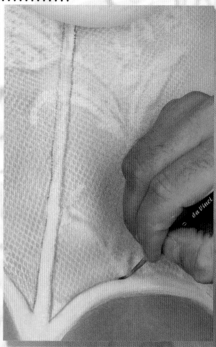

Auch bei den Verstrebungen und Rändern des Mieders können Sie zusätzlich mit dem Pinsel die Konturen verstärken.

You can additionally strengthen the contours of the bracing and the edges of the corsage with the same paintbrush.

STEP 19

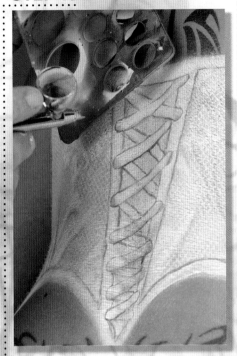

Mit einer Kreisschablone können Sie die Löcher der Schnürung optimieren. Mit einer geraden Schablone sprühen Sie leichte Schattierungen an der Schnürung ein.

You can optimize the eyelets of the cording with a circle stencil. With a straight stencil, spray a light shadow along the cording.

STEP 20

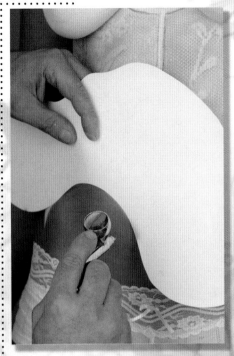

Damit sich das Mieder vom Körper noch ein wenig abhebt, sprühen Sie mit Grau einen Schatten an den Kanten entlang. Hilfreich dabei ist eine selbstgemachte Kurvenschablone aus Papier.

To visually lift the corsage off the body, spray shadings along the edges. A self-made paper stencil will be very helpful for this.

STEP 21

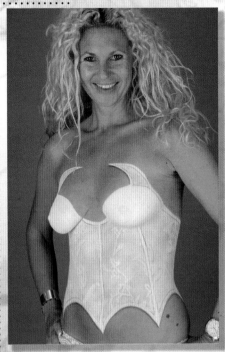

Hier ist die fertige Corsage. Sexy!

And here you go! The finished corsage. Sexy!

Künstler - Galerie
Artists' - Gallery

AIRBRUSH-BODYPAINTING IST MEIST nur ein Hobby oder ein Teil des künstlerischen Schaffens eines Künstlers. Umso erstaunlicher, wie viel Perfektion, Zeit und Mühe Bodypainter in ihre „vergänglichen" Werke investieren. In der Galerie finden Sie eine Auswahl internationaler Airbrush-Bodypainter. Lassen Sie sich von den Werken faszinieren und inspirieren!

AIRBRUSH BODY PAINTING IS MOSTLY A MERE hobby or a part of the artistic work of an artist. The more amazing it is how much perfection, time and effort the body painters invest into their "ephemeral" works. In the gallery you can see a selection of international body painters. Let their works fascinate and inspire you!

Paintings links/rechts: Bert Verstappen, www.bodypainteurope.com / Painting Mitte: Anja Pürkel, www.artandmake-up.de

GALERIE

Shahid Baig

Pakistan

Beauty of nature:
Spring and earth (2009)
Photo: Abdul Qayum

Violence and sin dominating peace (2009)
Photo: Abdul Qayum

Norbert Bauer

www.body-paint.at

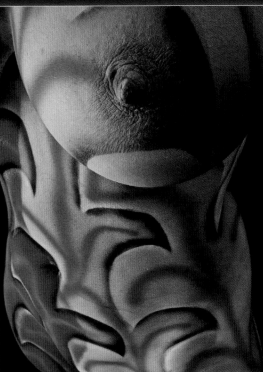

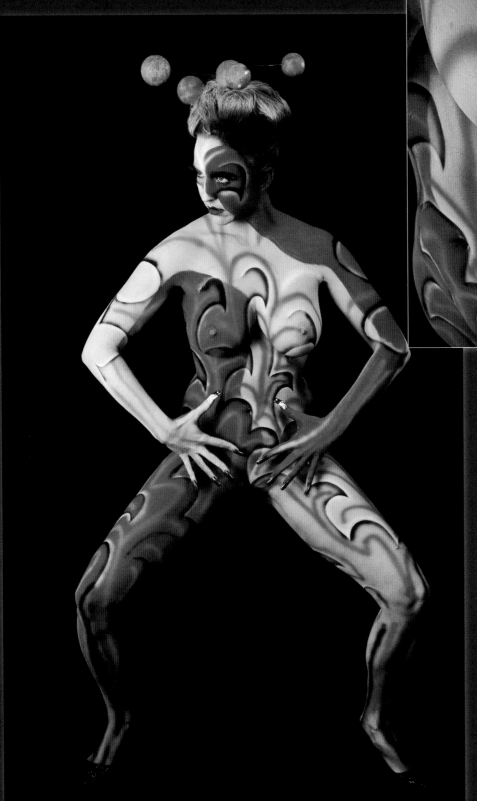

Blue Motion (2009)
Photo: Norbert Bauer

Herbie Betschart

www.airbrush-pur.ch

Model: Miriam
Photo: Urs Bachmann

Model: Miriam
Photo: Stefan Burkard

Anne-Kathrin Brexendorf

www.picassoline.de

Schutzengel-Sicherheit
Model: Bettina Hauer
Photo: Anne-Kathrin Brexendorf

Tiger (2008)
Model: Waltraud Thaler
Photo: Bettina Hauer

Claus Dirscherl

www.dirscherl-airbrush.de

Dragon
Model: MicHa (Michaela Haslauer)
Photo: Georg Schmitt - Photoart 1

Lava
Model: Marissa M. (Doris Mesko)
Photo: Willy Frimberger -
Body & Soul Photoworks

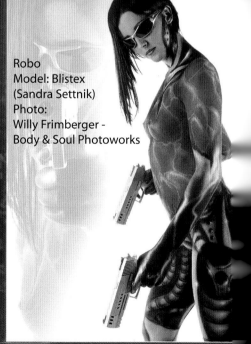

Robo
Model: Blistex
(Sandra Settnik)
Photo:
Willy Frimberger -
Body & Soul Photoworks

Christine Dumbsky

www.webparadise.com
www.body-paint.eu

Photos: Kurt Röhrken

Jörg Düsterwald

www.dewaldo.de

Isra Vison
Photo: Jörg Düsterwald

Musketiere
Photo: Tschiponnnique Skupin
www.future-image.de

Rotgelb
Photo: Studio C
Christine Gehrmann
www.fotostudioc.de

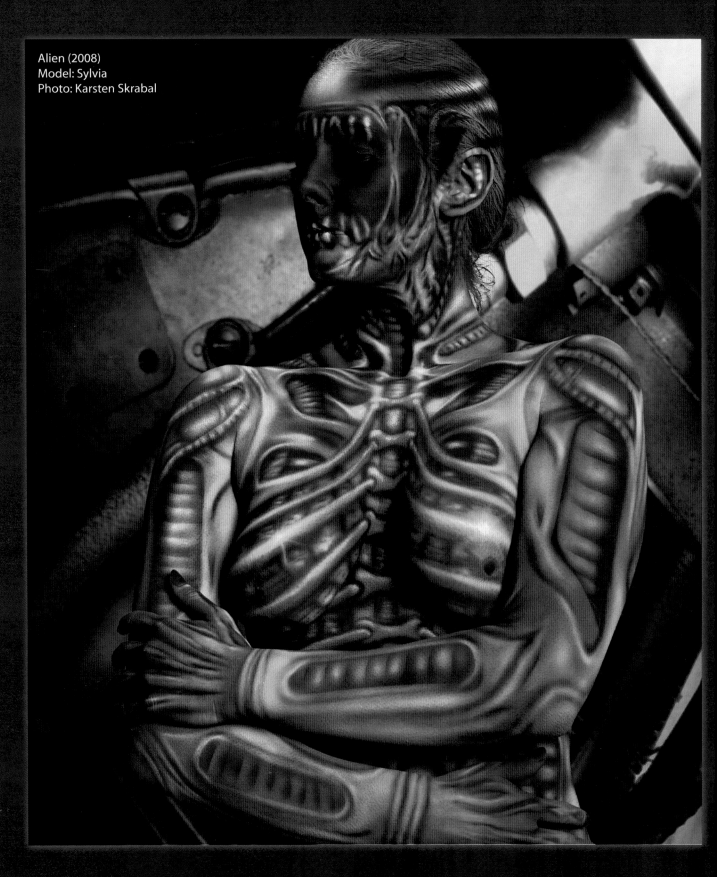

Alien (2008)
Model: Sylvia
Photo: Karsten Skrabal

Alex Hansen

www.alexhansenart.com

Private Painting (2007)
Model: Sylvia
Photo: Karsten Skrabal

Liza
Model: Liza
Photo: Viphoto

Sonnenuntergang
Model: Natascha
Photo: Viphoto

Zebra
Model: Marlene
Photo: Nadja Hluchovsky

Marcel Kuß

www.kuss-design.at

Karate Bodypainting (2007)
Team: Marcel Kuß und Katrin Höppl

Mozartkugel & Model (2006)
Model: Susanne
Photo: www.werbefotografie-rieger.com

Konstantin Militinskiy

www.bodyarttoday.com

Zodiac „Pisces"
Model: Julia Petrova
Photo: Konstantin Militinskiy

Impossible reality, inspired by René Magrittes
„Attempting the Impossible" (2003)
Model: Nina Boyko
Photo: Konstantin Militinskiy

Greece (2000)
Model: Juliya Rodionova
Photo: Konstantin Militinskiy

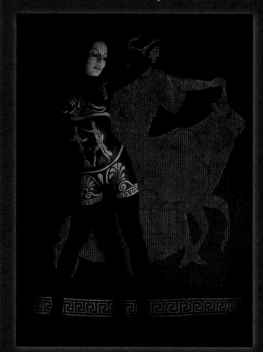

GALERIE

Alessandro Piva

www.lunaneraart.com

WBPF 2008
Team: Alessandro Rinaldi
Model: Chiara Piva,
Carmelo Bacchetta
Photo: Hans Joachim Heller

WBPF 2007
Model: Chiara Piva

Lothar Pötzl

www.lothar-poetzl.de

Model: Miriam

Model: Ulrike

GALERIE

BodypaintingCrew

Peter Richter, Janny Cierpka
www.bodypaintingcrew.com

(2008)
Team: Janny (Painting),
Peter (Prosthetic)

2004)
Team: Janny (Painting),
Peter (Prosthetic)

Burg (2002)
Team: Janny, Enrico, Peter
Model: Anja

Gegensätze unserer Zeit (2008)
Model: Kathleen
Photo: Foto-Studio Andrea Schumann

Petra und Peter Tronser

www.peter-tronser.de

WBPF 2008
1. Platz Special Effects Make-up
Model: Christina Seißler

Model: Michaela Haslauer

ANNO 10.2.2008

Ice
Model: Christina

Manfred Weißlein

www.atelier-weisslein.net

Moulin Rouge (2008)
Model: Kim
Team: Nicole Weinfurtner (Make-up, Hair),
Edith Wolf (Balloon Art)
Photo: Hans-Peter Burchardt

Fairy Dance - Elfentanz und Feenzauber (2008)
Model: Kim
Team: Nicole Weinfurtner (Make-up, Hair),
Edith Wolf (Balloon Art)
Photo: Hans-Peter Burchardt

Hommage to Hundertwasser (2005)
Model: Melanie
Photo: Hans-Peter Burchardt

Wolfgang Zack

www.wzack.de

GBPF 2007

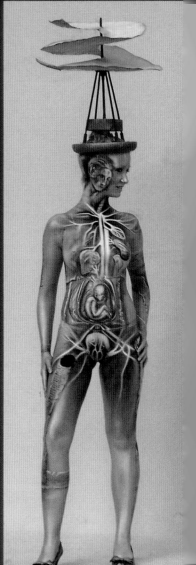

WBPF 2008
Team: Philipp Tronser
Model: Gloria

TIPPS & TROUBLESHOOTING

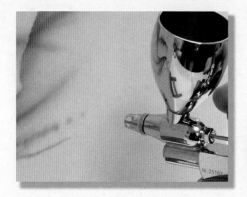

Problem	Lösung	Problem	Solution
Kompressor arbeitet nicht	• Überprüfen Sie, ob das Gerät einge-schaltet, das Netzkabel angeschlossen ist und ob die Steckdose Strom liefert	*Compressor doesn't work*	*• Check if compressor is switched on, plug it and check if electricity is available*
Kompressor wird heiß	• Gerät war zu lange im Betrieb oder die Kompressorleistung für die verwendete Düsengröße zu gering • Kompressor ausschalten und abkühlen lassen • Kompressor wechseln	*Compressor gets hot*	*• Has been working too long or its performance is too low for the applicated nozzle size* *• Switch off compressor and let cool down* *• Change compressor*
Airbrushgerät „sprenkelt" / liefert ein schlechtes Spritzbild	• Verschmutzte Nadel reinigen • Verbogene oder defekte Nadel austauschen • Verstopfte Nadelschutzkappe reinigen • Beschädigte Düse austauschen	*Airbrush device "sprinkles" / shows poor spraying characteristics*	*• Clean polluted needle* *• Replace bent or damaged needle* *• Clean clogged needle cap* *• Replace damaged nozzle*
Luft wird in den Farbnapf gedrückt (die Farbe sprudelt)	• Defekte Düse austauschen • Düse / Nadel herausnehmen, reinigen und wieder zusammensetzen • Beschädigte oder fehlende Düsendichtung erneuern • Luftkopf fester anschrauben	*Air is pressed in the paint cup (paint is bubbling)*	*• Replace damaged nozzle* *• Remove nozzle/needle, clean and insert again* *• Replace damaged or missing nozzle seal* *• Tighten the air head*
Das Airbrush-gerät versprüht keine Farbe	• Farbe nachfüllen • Verstopfte Düse reinigen • Nadelführung überprüfen und Nadelfeststeller anziehen, um Nadelbewegung zu ermöglichen • Verstopften Farbflaschenanschluss reinigen, Loch oder Ansaugröhrchen durchpieksen • Zähflüssige Farbe stärker verdünnen	*The airbrush device does not spray any paint*	*• Top up the paint.* *• Clean clogged nozzle.* *• Check needle guidance and tighten needle securing to enable needle movement* *• Clean clogged paint bottle connector, prick hole or suction tube* *• Thin more the pasty paint*
Farbe bröckelt am Körper	• Farbaufbau korrigieren: Weniger Farbe / Farbschichten auftragen • Der Farbe Glyzerin beimischen • Haut zu fettig, zuvor keine Lotion verwenden	*Paint crumbles on the body*	*• Adjust paint composition: Spray less paint/paint layers* *• Add glycerin to the paint* *• Skin is too greasy, do not use lotion before*
Farbe läuft am Körper herunter	• Farbe weniger verdünnen • Weniger Farbe auftragen (Hebel nicht so weit zurückziehen, mehr Abstand vom Körper)	*Paint runs from the body*	*• Do not thin paint so much* *• Apply less pain (do not draw back the lever so far increase distance from the body)*

AIRBRUSH & BODYPAINTING LINKS

Airbrushgeräte/ Kompressoren
Airbrush devices/ compressors

Badger/Vega
www.badgerairbrush.com

Createx
www.createx.de

Efbe
www.efbe-airbrush.de

Harder & Steenbeck
www.harder-airbrush.de

Holbein
www.holbein-airbrush.de

Iwata
www.airbrush-iwata.com

Paasche
www.paascheairbrush.com

Rich
www.honsell-artproducts.de

RichPen
www.richpen.com

SATA
www.sata.com

Sparmax
www.sparmax.com.tw

Farben
Paints

AviTaN
www.effect-color.eu

Badger
www.badgerairbrush.com

Diamond FX
www.diamondfx.eu

Eulenspiegel
www.eulenspiegel.de

Fardel
www.fardel.com

Mehron
www.mehron.com

Kryolan
www.kryolan.de

Paasche
www.paascheairbrush.com

Senjo-Tattoo
www.senjo-tattoo.de

SprayOn
www.airbrush-makeup.de

Mist-Air
www.mist-air.com

Temptu
www.temptu.com

Yucantan
www.spray-tanning.de

Zeitschriften
Magazines

Airbrush Step by Step
www.airbrush-magazin.de

Illusion Magazine
www.illusionmagazine.co.uk

Brush Strokes Magazine
www.brushstrokesmag.com

Verbände
Associations

World Body Painting Association
www.wbpa.info

FACE – The Face Painting Association
www.facepaint.co.uk

BODDYPAINTING EVENTS

	World Bodypainting Festival	www.bodypainting-festival.com
	Body Art Festival	www.body-art.be
	Swiss Bodypainting Day	www.swissbodypaintingday.ch
	German Bodypainting Festival	www.german-bodypainting-festival.de
	Festival der Farben	www.festivalofcolours.com
	Italian Bodypainting Festival	www.italianbodypaintingfestival.it
	Riga Body Painting Festival	www.stilistuskola.lv
	Maskerade	www.maskerade.org
	Fantasy-Worldwide Festival	www.fw-contest.com
	Moscow Tattoo- and Bodyart Festival	www.moscowbodyartfestival.com
	Stockholm Bodypainting Contest	www.makeupinstitute.com/SBPC/
	Odessa Body Art Carnival	www.odessa-guide.com
	UK Body Painting Festival	www.ukbodypaintingfestival.co.uk
	UK Face & Body Painting Convention	www.facepaintingconvention.co.uk
	Welsh International Face and Bodypainting Festival	www.welshfaceandbodypaintingfestival.co.uk

IMATS International make-up artist trade show
wechselnde Veranstaltungsorte
changing locations

www.makeupartistshow.net

PHOTO INDEX

S/P	Info
2/3	Photo: Mist-Air
4	1) Painting: Pashur, Photo: Mehron 2+3) Photo: Roger Hassler 4) Painting: Gaëlle Mouster, Photo: Roger Hassler
5	1) Painting + Photo: Nadja Hluchovsky, Model: Marlene 2) Painting: Herbie Betschart, Model: Miriam, Photo: Martin Rahn
6	1-3) Photos: istockphoto 4) Painting: Anne-Kathrin Brexendorf Model: Katja Famschanz, Photo: Bettina Hauer 5) Painting: Alessandro Piva, Team: Alessandro Rinaldi, Model: Chiara Piva 6) Photo: Mist-Air
7	1) Painting: Roger Hassler, Model: Dajana, Photo: Claus Döpelheuer 2) Painting: Roger Hassler, Model: Nicole, Photo: Claus Döpelheuer
8	1-2) Photos: Roger Hassler (GBPF 2008) 3) Painting+Photo: Bruno Leyser
9	1) Photo: Roger Hassler (WBPF 2007) 2) Painting + Photo: Konstantin Militinskiy, Model: Tatiana Parhomenko
10	1) Make-up: Anne-Kathrin Brexendorf 2) istockphoto 3) Painting: Janny, Bodypainting Crew, Hair: Uschi
11	Photo: Roger Hassler
12	Painting: Udo Schurr, Photo: Roger Hassler (WBPF 2007)
13	Painting: Alessandro Piva, Model: Chiara Piva
14	Painting: Roger Hassler, Model: Dajana, Photo: Claus Döpelheuer
15-17	PR-Photos: Badger, Harder & Steenbeck, Hansa, Efbe, Gabbert, Paasche, Uslu Airlines
18-19	Photos: Roger Hassler
20-21	PR-Photos: Harder & Steenbeck, Efbe
22-23	PR-Photos: Harder & Steenbeck, Efbe, Createx, Honsell
24	PR-Photos: Harder & Steenbeck, Iwata
25-29	Photos: Roger Hassler
30	1) Painting: Pashur, Photo: Mehron 2) PR-Photos: Mehron, Kryolan
31	1) Painting: Pashur, Photo: Mehron 2) PR-Photo: Eulenspiegel
32-39	PR-Photos: siehe Firmennennung / see company name on page
40-43	Painting + Photos: Roger Hassler
44	1-2) Painting + Photos: Roger Hassler 3-4) Photos: Roger Hassler (GBPF 2008)
45	1) Photo: Roger Hassler 2) Photo: Mist-Air
46-53	Painting + Photos: Roger Hassler
54	Photo: Temptu
55	1) Photo: Mist-Air 2) Photo: Roger Hassler 3-5) Mist-Air
56-58	Photos: Roger Hassler
59-63	Painting: Oliver Heiden, Photo: Claus Döpelheuer
64-65	1) Temptu 2-4) PR-Photos: Temptu, Kryolan, Mehron
66-67	Make-up: Roger Hassler, Photo: Claus Döpelheuer

S/P	Info
68	Photo: istockphoto
69-70	1) Mist-Air 2) Photo: istockphoto 3) Mist-Air 4) Photo: istockphoto
71	Photos: istockphoto
72	Painting: Roger Hassler, Model: Dajana, Photo: Claus Döpelheuer
73	1-2) Painting+Photos: Roger Hassler 3) Photo: Mehron
74	1) Photo: Roger Hassler (WBPF 2007) 2) Painting: Fredi Schmidt, Photo: Roger Hassler (WBPF 2007) 3) Photo: Roger Hassler (WBPF 2007)
75	1+3) Painting: Roger Hassler, Model: Dajana, Photo: Claus Döpelheuer 2) Painting: Roger Hassler, Model: Nicole, Photo: Claus Döpelheuer
76-87	Painting: Roger Hassler, Model: Dajana, Photo: Claus Döpelheuer
88-95	Painting: Roger Hassler, Model: Dajana, Photo: Claus Döpelheuer
96-105	Painting: Roger Hassler, Model: Nicole, Photo: Claus Döpelheuer
106-117	Painting: Roger Hassler, Model: Dajana, Photo: Claus Döpelheuer
118-127	Painting: Roger Hassler, Model: Dajana, Photo: Claus Döpelheuer
128-135	Painting: Oliver Heiden, Photo: Claus Döpelheuer
136-155	Paintings + Photos: siehe Bildbeschriftung / see names on page
156	Paintings + Photos: Roger Hassler
157	1) Photos: Claus Döpelheuer 2) PR-Photos: Mehron, Fardel 3) PR-Fotos: Airbrush Step by Step, Illusion Publishing
158	1) Photo: Roger Hassler (WBPF 2007) 2) Painting: Bruno Leyser, Photo: Roger Hassler (GBPF 2008) 3) Photo: Roger Hassler (GBPF 2008)

Verwendete Abkürzungen / *Abbreviations:*

GBPF: German Bodypainting Festival
WBPF: World Bodypainting Festival

Wir danken allen Paintern, Modellen und Fotografen für ihre freundliche Genehmigung und Unterstützung.

We thank all painters, models and photographers for their courtesy and assistance.

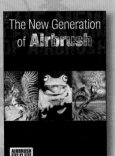

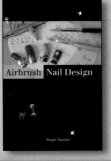